THINK
Feel
Speak
Write

D O 2.0

A Path Toward Realizing Your Purpose

R. LEE MOORE, SR.

Cover design and book layout
One Creative Mind, LLC
ISBN: 979-8-9905229-2-3

Dedication

When I look back on my life's journey,
I think about the people I've met along the way.
Your impact, inspiration and instruction have
shaped who I am today.

A sincere thanks to my ancestors, family,
friends and those special individuals who have
encouraged me to keep pushing during the
tough times and celebrated with me in times
of triumph.

Most especially I thank my Creator who set
me on the path to discover who I am, find,
pursue my divine purpose... and fulfill it.

— *R. Lee Moore, Sr.*

Contents

Introduction

Since the release of "Think, Feel, Speak, Write – Do" in 2011, my life has been a journey filled with transformative experiences. After devoting several years to caring for my mother until her passing in 2012, I relocated to a small town near Philadelphia, where I embarked on a decade long role as caregiver of my currently 103-year-old aunt.

These life-changing events, along with others, have led me to cherish and apply the principles outlined in this book. Thus, I am delighted to introduce "Think, Feel, Speak, Write – Do 2.0: A Path Toward Realizing Your Purpose."

On a personal level, I have witnessed firsthand the profound impact of these principles in shaping my own life. Within this "info-novel," I share stories that provide readers with a fresh perspective on the consequences that arise when these principles are either embraced or overlooked on one's life journey.

By understanding the interconnections of thinking, feeling, speaking, and writing, I have successfully pursued my unique life's purpose – inspiring others to break free from conventional notions of success and embrace a life of extraordinary significance. This book acts as a transformative exploration into the essence of living a purpose-driven life. By following the core principles outlined within, you will embark on a quest to unlock your full potential and bring your divine purpose to fruition.

I warmly invite you to join me on this voyage of self-discovery and self-transformation. By fully embracing these principles, you will experience subtle yet profound shifts that will guide you towards a life rich in meaning, purpose, and fulfillment.

May this book light your path as you strive to lead an authentic life aligned with your true self. As you delve into the wisdom within these pages and connect with the shared narratives, may you awaken to the limitless potential within you and boldly embrace the unique purpose that awaits.

Warm Regards,

R. Lee Moore, Sr.

*"Live Life with Purpose
& Passion!"*

Chapter 1

THINK

Think [1]

- to have a conscious mind, to some extent of reasoning, remembering experiences, making rational decisions.

- to have a certain thing as the subject of one's thoughts.

- to call something to one's conscious mind.

- to consider something as a possible action, choice, etc.

- to invent or conceive of something.

"I think I will..."

How many times have we repeated that phrase in a day? "I think I'd better get up now and get ready for work." That casual thought begins the process of our legs moving to get out of bed and begin doing what we normally do to prepare for another day on the job. But as suddenly as that thought enters our mind, another opposing thought quickly replaces it with, "But I think I'll just lay here for a few more minutes." Our legs instantly turn to jelly and our body relaxes as if being massaged by its own private massage therapist. Our mind is fantastic and fickle.

Thinking begins every action we perform

Even when we automatically act without a conscious thought, thinking happens first. Scratching an itch, coughing when the inside of our throat is tickled or even laughing at what seems funny, all happen after a thought is produced in our mind. No one acts without thinking! "I wasn't thinking" is an expression we use to define something dumb we may have done or said. In fact, you were thinking, only about something other than what you should have been thinking of. Remarkably, our mind never stops producing thoughts.

Our mind, which resides in our brain, protected by our skull produces innumerable thoughts without a single pause. Experts estimate that we can have over 1,200 conscious or unconscious thoughts a day while still others estimate even higher numbers. While thinking is produced inside our mind, we know those thoughts go out into an unseen dimension to continue their work mysteriously and silently.

We are not aware of the tremendous task a thought performs on behalf of its originator. A thought enters our mind and when fully formed, begins to produce results, whether we like it or not, whether we are aware of the consequences or not, or whether it serves our best interest or not. It does what we think. Thoughts are things that act on our behalf.

> *"Our mind is*
> ***fantastic*** *and fickle."*

Our brain is an astonishing organ. We may never utilize nor understand the full capacity of what we may accomplish if we were to fully use it. The debate rages on whether we use 10% or more of our brain. Certainly, that is an interesting discussion. However, what is more significant is the fact that we have an unlimited capacity to learn. Our brains can never become so full of information or data that it is no longer able to continue storing information, unlike even the largest computer hard drives.

Because our brain is so uniquely and fantastically made, doesn't it make sense that the functioning part of our brain, namely our mind and the thoughts it produces, are no less incredible in nature?

> "*Think about things that are*
> *excellent*
> *and worthy of praise.*"

Since we are created in the image, likeness, or reflection of our Creator, we should do something like what He does; we should co-create! We imagine great and wonderful things, draw the plans, consider the costs, and build what we imagined into a physical reality. But our creative "powers" do not end with what our hands can produce. Thoughts that our mind has produced have materialized into events and deeds. We create situations and circumstances all the time, but we seldom credit or recognize them as being a product of our thoughts.

Ever notice when you have constant thoughts of being late, things begin to happen to cause you to be late? You cannot find an article of clothing, your keys or wallet; the public transportation is later than usual; all the slower drivers end up in front of you; you cannot find a parking space, and on and on. Yes, concentrating on being late creates the thoughts that go on a mission to create lateness on our behalf. We should concentrate on being on time.

I am sure we all, at one time or another, have had someone on our mind that we just could not stop thinking about. Eventually, our phone rings and who would be on the other end? That person about whom we were thinking! Thoughts can function as messengers. Be careful what messages you are sending.

Thoughts create

Our mind creates thoughts that go out and make the picture we imagined into reality. Ever hear a noise at home late at night in the dark? Our mind tells us something or someone is in our house or room and will do us harm when it finds us. We begin to see the danger in our thoughts and produce a scene no less dramatic than one performed on a Broadway stage. Our heart beats faster, the adrenaline starts to flow; we look for weapons for protection or scheme an escape route if we must run! Already you are thinking, "How fast and far can I run?" "Don't make me come out there and hurt somebody!"

Our mind created a thought that produced a fearful disposition, whether real danger was imminent or not. Tell me, why doesn't a strange noise in your home late at night ever mean that someone is there to leave the keys to a brand-new car or a stack of money on your night stand? Imagine that instead.

> *"You are worthy and*
> *valuable.*
> *Think that instead."*

If we realized how powerful our thoughts were, we might be more careful what we think. We would protect our head, consider what we feed our brand and better control the thoughts that come from our mind. We would use our mind more often to think positive, productive thoughts that would serve us and others well.

We would send positive, wholesome, and helpful thoughts out into the universe instead of negative, harmful, counter-productive thoughts. Indeed, the United Negro College Fund's motto says it all, "A mind is a terrible thing to waste!"

> *"A Mind is a terrible thing to waste!"*

The Apostle Paul says in Philippians 4:8, *"And now, dear brothers and sisters, one final thing. Fix your thoughts on what is true, and honorable, and right, and pure, and lovely, and admirable. Think about things that are excellent and worthy of praise."*

Paul must have known that the power of thought pushes us toward our purpose, rather than pulls us away from our God-given destiny.

Our mind can think all sorts of thoughts, from belly-laughing humor to gut-wrenching tragedy. We think thoughts of our past and present with the same ease with which we think about our future. We think correct, accurate thoughts as well as thoughts that are wrong and inaccurate, sometimes without ever noticing the difference between the two.

Sometimes our wrong thoughts become our dominant thoughts that go out and accomplish a task with the same intensity as if they were right. Our thoughts, right or wrong, when allowed to run wild, will accomplish their end, whether we want them to or not.

Private thoughts of "I'm stupid or unworthy" create conditions for errors and inferior positions in life. We are what we think – not what others think, but what we THINK others think of us. We send out thought messages that say, "Don't choose me, I'm unworthy" or "Don't trust me, I'm a failure."

Our thoughts produce actions that support and confirm our incorrect thinking.

"No matter what I do, I can't get ahead."
"If I have all that I really want,
people will be jealous of me."
"No one loves me for myself."
"Everybody can't be rich; there isn't
enough money for everyone."
"It is what it is!"

Although these thoughts are not true, some think these to themselves daily, confirming their negative message. Thoughts are creative, whether they are right or wrong.

Thoughts can make you sick

The right side of our brain contains the impulses to imagine or visualize. We visualize or perceive the world around us through our thoughts. Events that take place are viewed as positive or negative depending on our perception or imagination. If thoughts are positive, our outlook on the world will be positive, giving us a happy and healthy physical environment.

Negative thoughts can be the central cause of many ailments in our physical body. When our thoughts cause us to be stressed, our bodies become physically tense, which produces a condition of unease or dis-ease (disease).

Any negative thought repeated over and over again can become part of our framework and manifest itself physically, either in the form of pain or disease. [1]Studies have pinpointed some of the ailments and diseases associated with particular thoughts:

- Bearing the brunt of others - *ankle pain*
- Overly concerned about future - *right shoulder pain*
- Holding to past traumas - *left shoulder pain*
- Turmoil in relationships - *pain in the thighs*
- Inability to adapt to new circumstances - *knee pain*
- Excessive anger - *recurrent fever*
- Emotional problems and melancholy - *heart problems*
- Extreme need to control situations and dominate people - *diabetes*
- Confusion and indecisiveness - *migraines*
- Emotional insecurities and fear of rejection - *obesity*
- Personal and financial insecurities - *low back pain*
- Resentments and feeling of guilt - *cancer*

The list goes on and on. Whether you agree or disagree with these conclusions, it is still a proven fact that extreme and continuous negative thoughts can cause physical damage to one's body. We say stress is what causes illnesses, when actually it is stressful thoughts.

Thoughts can kill

Negative thoughts, even if never verbally expressed, will work powerfully against any purpose we may have been born to fulfill. Some have missed their God-appointed life's purpose because of thoughts of inferiority or believing what others have said about them instead of what God had ordained.

Negative thoughts can kill the most hopeful dreams, destroy the best of intentions, and ruin wonderful relationships. "I thought I could say anything to you and you would understand." "I would try that, but I don't think I'm good at business." "I don't think I would do well in school, so I should probably just look for a job." "I don't think they love me any more, since I've gained so much weight." "I don't think I'm the one whom God has chosen to do something like that." "Why, what would people think?"

> *"Negative thoughts can kill dreams."*

The world is presently without some wonderful teachers, biologists, writers, entrepreneurs, musicians, lawyers, scientists, poets, chemists, carpenters, artists, judges, fathers, singers, doctors, accountants, mothers, photographers, pastors, counselors, police officers, athletes, respiratory therapists, engineers, pharmacists, human services workers, husbands, wives, and a host of other tremendous people who have never reached their potential because they allowed their thoughts to chase their greatness away. Is your unfulfilled purpose on the list?

The story of Moses after he sees the burning bush is an example of what can happen when our thoughts negate even God's unmistakable appointment for our lives.

> *"We are responsible for our thoughts."*

Exodus 4:10-13 reads, *"But Moses pleaded with the Lord, "O Lord, I'm not very good with words. I never have been, and I'm not now, even though you have spoken to me. I get tongue-tied, and my words get tangled."*

Then the Lord asked Moses, "Who makes a person's mouth? Who decides whether people speak or do not speak, hear or do not hear, see or do not see? Is it not I, the Lord? Now go! I will be with you as you speak, and I will instruct you in what to say." But Moses again pleaded, "Lord, please! Send anyone else."

Indeed Moses had a speech problem. He was probably teased as a child, seen as "different" and perhaps considered a bit strange because of his stutter or lack of eloquence. His experience with greatness in Egypt, his encounter with the supernaturally burning bush, and even direct conversation with the Great I AM could not override his dominant thought of inadequacy. It was even difficult for God to convince him that his inability to speak was separate from his availability to serve.

The more we repeat negative thoughts, the more they are ingrained in our minds and become a permanent part of our belief system. Negative thoughts repeated will prevent positive outcomes.

These thoughts, blockages, and self-sabotaging affirmations are lies that we *believe* to be true. They get proven over and over again as we live them out. This type of thinking is habitual and will continue to be reinforced as long as we keep it up. You are worthy and valuable. *Try thinking that instead.*

Thoughts attract

Have you ever considered thoughts are things that attract like magnets? There is an unseen force that mysteriously draws to you the thing you are constantly thinking of. This "thing" may not be what you actually want, but is a product of a sustained thought that keeps playing over and over again in your mind. "I'm always broke; I never have enough money." You don't want to be without means and would much rather have access to the necessary resources you need. However, your thoughts of lack and want will continue to attract those conditions until you change the script.

"No one cares about me. No one likes me." This is a driving thought that chases friends and family away from you with the same intensity as thinking self-affirming thoughts can attract people to you.

"I'll never be anything in life." Like ordering a well-prepared meal, repeated negative thoughts will deliver to you an empty platter of opportunities, dead-end jobs, and an endless stream of empty promises and disappointing appointments.

I don't understand how thoughts attract anymore than I understand how hydrogen and oxygen, when combined in their proper parts, result in the production of water. Yet, we use water everyday without question, as do we consistently think thoughts that attract the good or the bad. Our thoughts are stored in a sort of "escrow" until they are activated by our strong, deep desire to see them materialize. Some call that "wishful thinking"; I call it believing in your heart, otherwise known as faith.

Where thoughts come from

Our thoughts can originate from the experiences of our childhood. Crisis situations, frightening episodes or abusive conditions that have been pushed back into our subconscious resurface as negative thinking. These negative thoughts cripple nearly every area of our life, as they play continuous refrains of failure, inferiority or fear of revealing our true self.

> *"Change the way you think."*

Our thoughts also come from all the data we store in our brain and process in our mind. This data or information comes from everything we see and hear. Radio and television programming, MP3s, videos, books, magazines, advertisements, events, people, places and stories all provide combined experiences that shape our thoughts.

With a constant barrage of negative information, we go about our day rehearsing thoughts of recession, joblessness, crime and violence, uprisings and war. No wonder it's difficult to believe God has created us to be a positive influence on society. We have become much too dulled in our thinking to hear from God or even care. Apathy is now the new norm.

This is why we should be careful what we feed our mind and even more importantly, what we allow to enter the minds of our children. We allow the media to give our children not just information, but also a way of life. Instead of feeding them God's vision, we allow them to receive the "tele's" vision. This may be one of the reasons why real vision and purpose is so lacking amongst the youth in our communities. Their thoughts are immersed in the world's idea of what life should be. It is apparent in what they talk about, what they desire to have, the clothes they wear, the music they listen to and the lack of ambition they display.

Romans 12:2 tells us, *"Don't copy the behavior and customs of this world, but let God transform you into a new person by changing the way you think. Then you will learn to know God's will for you, which is good and pleasing and perfect."*

We may not be totally aware of how much the world's views influence our thinking. That is why we want what we don't need, buy what we can't afford and do what others do. We have been shaped by what we see and hear. We can act no other way because our mind is conditioned to think as the world thinks.

No matter how hard we try to do differently, we find ourselves conforming to the world's standards that are dictated to us. Our clothing reflects our culture. Heels that are so high they hurt and pants that are so low they border indecent exposure are deemed as "fashionable," and so we wear them.

We have become a world of followers, not leaders. We follow the followers repeating the same events and circumstances as those before us, hardly ever thinking for ourselves. We blindly follow customs and traditions without realizing their purpose or original intent.

There is a story of a young child who sees her mother cutting off the end of a ham and discarding it before putting it in the roasting pan and asks, "Mom, why do you cut the end of the ham off before putting it in the oven?" "I don't know," mom responds, "I believe it helps to cook more evenly. But go ask your grandmother."

And so she seeks her granny's council. "Grandma, why does my mom cut the end of the ham off before she puts it in the oven?" "Hmmm," Grandma ponders, "it allows the juices to flow through for better flavor?" Again her question is passed to an older, much-wiser matriarch. "Ask my mother, your great-grandmother. She will know."

Finally, the child finds the originator of the ham tradition. "Grandma-ma, why do we cut off the end of the ham before putting it in the oven? Does it taste better that way?"

"Oh sweetie," great-grand mom replies. And with a loving twinkle in her aged eyes, she solves the mystery of the sacred ritual. "I did that years ago because *my roasting pan was too small.*"

Why do we do what we do? Think about it. Do you know where the traditions you follow come from? It may be worth your while to investigate and find out.

Many have found after years of living that their lives were not completely their own. They have followed those who have followed others before them without thinking.

Actually, they were thinking. "I should do what they did because it served them well." That is a true statement. It did serve them well. However, we each have a purpose that fits us in a unique and personal way. We must change our thinking to know the path that is good, pleasing and perfect for us today. *(See Romans 12:2)*

By changing our thinking, we can change the direction of our lives. Doing things differently makes us feel better for a moment, but an effective change will happen when our mind is reshaped to think positively.

Thinking begins every action we perform. All actions are controlled by the thoughts formed in our mind. We can change our mind, and we can change our thoughts. We must understand it is our responsibility to think thoughts that support our purpose in life. We must be diligent to guard what enters our mind by guarding what we see and hear.

Thoughts create our reality. As difficult as this may be to understand, it is a fact that from birth our lives are shaped by our thoughts. Our mind is capable of thinking all sorts of thoughts – both positive and negative – that ultimately create the circumstances in which we live.

Thoughts can make us physically sick, and can kill our hopes and dreams. Many of the things that appear in our lives, welcomed or not, are attracted by our thoughts. The more we think on purpose and with passion, the more we attract the things that God has intended for us.

In the upcoming story, observe the transformative power of Darnel's thoughts as they guide him from a place of darkness into the light. Explore further...

Beyond the Shadows

D arnel leaned back in his chair, the creaking of the old wood a familiar sound in the small, dimly lit maintenance office at the University of Pennsylvania. It was his break time, and he idly scrolled through Instagram, a pastime that had become his escape from the drudgery of his job. At forty-eight, Darnel felt stuck. Stuck in a job he did not care for, stuck in a cycle of negativity, and stuck in a life that seemed to pale in comparison to his sister Katrina's.

Growing up, their household had been a constant reminder of his perceived inadequacies. His father, a demanding man with a sharp tongue, never hesitated to point out Darnel's flaws.

"Darnel, why can't you be more like Katrina?" his father would often say, his voice dripping with disappointment. "She's top of her class, going places. And you? What are you doing with your life?"

Katrina, the golden child, had been showered with praise and encouragement. She excelled at everything she touched, from academics to sports, and eventually went on to Temple Law School. Today, she was a partner at a prestigious law firm in Philadelphia, a shining star in the family's eyes. Meanwhile, Darnel had drifted from one menial job to another, never finding his footing or earning the same admiration.

His mother, passive and quiet, never intervened. She would sit silently as his father berated him, offering only a sad, knowing look that did little to comfort him.

"Darnel, you know your father just wants the best for you," she would say weakly, though her words rang hollow.

The years had not been kind. Darnel's life was a series of disappointments: two failed marriages, three children he barely saw, and a job as a mainte-nance worker that he had held for eighteen years. His self-esteem had plummeted, and he had turned to alcohol and recreational marijuana to numb the pain. Conversations with his coworkers revolved around the latest gossip or reality TV shows, the only subjects that sparked his interest anymore. He often clashed with his long-time coworker Brandon over sports and women, their arguments a thin veil for their own frustrations.

"Darnel, you're just a bitter old man," Brandon said during one heated exchange about their favorite football teams. "No wonder your life's a mess."

"At least I'm not living in a fantasy world, thinking my team's going to win the Super Bowl," Darnel shot back, his words laced with anger.

One evening, as Darnel sat in his small, cluttered apartment, a particular Instagram ad caught his eye. It was about improving one's life through developing a positive pattern of thinking. Intrigued, he clicked on it. The speaker's words resonated with something deep inside him, something that had been buried under years of self-doubt and negativity.

"Your thoughts shape your reality. Change your thoughts, and you change your life," the speaker said.

Darnel began to listen to similar postings, his curiosity growing with each video. Over the next few weeks, he immersed himself in articles, podcasts, and motivational talks about positive thinking. Slowly, he started to apply the principles he learned. He wrote affirmations, practiced gratitude, and made a conscious effort to shift his mind-set.

One day, Brandon noticed a change in him. "Darnel, what's going on with you? You seem different."

"I've been listening to some stuff about positive thinking," Darnel replied, surprised at how natural it felt to share this. "It's really been helping."

"Positive thinking, huh?" Brandon said skeptically. "Well, whatever you're doing, keep it up. You seem... happier."

Darnel smiled, a real, genuine smile that felt foreign on his face. "Thanks, man."

And then, something fantastic happened. A fantastic opportunity arose at the university. There was an announcement about free night classes in business management, available to employees. Darnel hesitated at first, the old voices of doubt whispering that he was not good enough, that he could not do it. But the new voices, the positive ones he had been nurturing, encouraged him to take the leap.

"You have nothing to lose and everything to gain," he told himself, repeating one of his new affirmations.

He enrolled in the classes and found that he enjoyed them. He was good at it, too. The concepts made sense, and he felt a spark of ambition that had been dormant for so long. For the first time in years, Darnel felt hopeful.

Six months later, Darnel had completed the courses. His performance and newfound attitude caught the attention of his supervisors. They offered him a position in the facilities management office, a job with upward mobility and a significant pay increase.

"Darnel, we've been impressed with your progress," his supervisor said during the meeting where he was offered the new position. "We believe you have the potential to go far here."

"Thank you," Darnel replied, almost choking on his emotions. "I won't let you down."

With his new job, Darnel's life began to change dramatically. He met someone special, a kind-hearted woman named Lisa who worked in the university's administrative office. They hit it off immediately, sharing a love for music and a passion for helping others.

"Darnel, you're one of the most genuine people I've ever met," Lisa said one evening as they walked through the campus gardens. "I can't believe how lucky I am to have found you."

"I feel the same way," Darnel replied, his heart full. "You've brought so much light into my life."

They got married in a small, intimate ceremony, surrounded by friends and family. His sister Katrina was unfortunately away on a lecture and couldn't attend on such short notice. For the first time, Darnel felt genuinely happy, truly at peace. He also made a concerted effort to reconnect with his children. He took responsibility for his past mistakes and worked to build a better relationship with them.

"Dad, it's really great to see you trying," his eldest son, Michael, said during a family outing. "We missed you."

"I missed you too, buddy," Darnel tearfully replied. "I'm going to make it right, I promise."

Thinking in a more positive, productive manner, and developing a better self-image helped Darnel overcome the negative reinforcement of his parents. It enabled him to lead a more fulfilling life. He realized that his past did not define him, and that he had the power to change his future.

One day, as he walked through the university campus, he ran into Katrina, who was there to give a lecture at the law school. "Darnel, you look different," she said, studying him with a mix of surprise and admiration. "Happier. What is changed?"

"A lot, actually," Darnel replied, smiling. "I've been working on myself, thinking more positively. It's made a huge difference."

"I'm really proud of you," Katrina said, her voice sincere. "I always knew you had it in you."

Hearing those words from his sister, the one who had always been the benchmark, filled Darnel with a sense of validation he had long craved. He hugged her tightly, feeling a weight lift off his shoulders.

"Thanks, Katrina. That means a lot," he said, his voice choked with emotion.

As the years passed, Darnel continued to grow both personally and professionally. He advanced in his new career, finding fulfillment in his work and pride in his accomplishments. His relationship with Lisa flourished, and his bond with his children strengthened.

Looking back, Darnel saw his life as a journey of transformation. From the shadow of his sister's success and the negativity of his upbringing, he had emerged stronger, wiser, and more confident. He realized that the key to his happiness had always been within him, waiting to be unlocked by a shift in perspective. Darnel stood on the porch of his home one evening, watching the sunset with Lisa by his side. He felt a deep sense of gratitude for the journey he had undertaken and the life he had built.

"Lisa, do you ever think about how different things could have been?" he asked, his voice contemplative.

"Sometimes," she replied, squeezing his hand. "But I'm glad things turned out this way. We've created a beautiful life together."

"Yeah, we have," Darnel said, smiling as he watched the sky change colors. "And I'm finally at peace with who I am."

In the end, Darnel learned that the power of positive thinking and self-belief could transform even the most difficult of lives. He had found his way out of the shadows, and into the light, where he belonged.

"I think I will..."

THINK FEEL SPEAK WRITE- DO

Chapter 2

Feel

Feel [1]

- undergo an emotional sensation or be in a particular state of mind: "She felt resentful."

- find: come to believe on the basis of emotion, intuitions or indefinite grounds: "I feel that he doesn't like me."

- have a feeling or perception about one self in reaction to someone's behavior or attitude: "She felt small and insignificant."

- an intuitive awareness: "It's easy when you get the feel of it."

- produce a certain impression: "It feels nice to be home again."

"I feel that something is happening!"

Emotions and feelings are intangible, invisible things that can manifest in a physical manner. Whether you feel a certain way because of what you think, or you feel that way because of what you, physically experience, the results will be the same.

Emotions have a major influence on the thoughts you have, both positively and negatively. Emotions or feelings attached to a thought function as an engine. It activates that thought in an unusual way. It seems to drive that thought into reality in a way that does not happen when feelings or emotions are not present.

The more enthusiastic the thought and the more intense the emotion associated with that thought, the greater the impact that thought will have on a person's circumstances. When extreme anger is present with a thought, extremely negative events are likely to happen. When enthusiastic, loving thoughts are dominant, positive situations effortlessly engulf a person's life.

When you wake up in the middle of the night with thoughts of the security of your home on your mind, you will go back to sleep if there are no feelings or emotions attached to the thoughts. But if your thoughts are associated with fear, you may not go back to sleep for hours. In fact, you may get up and check the doors and windows, even waking those close to you or calling someone, including the police, until the fear subsides.

> *"Emotions influence our thoughts."*

However, the same is true when you wake up with joy and comfort as the dominant feelings about your safety. You will feel extremely secure with joy flowing through the thought of being in your home. You may even roll over with a smile on your face. Neither scenario is dependent on the quality of the security system, but rather the feeling that produces the thought about security.

When sadness surrounds you, your thoughts become dark and jaded. Depression and the inability to function sets in. Eventually, your purpose for living becomes dim and worthless.

Emotions and feelings are related to thought

Not all thoughts, however, cause a feeling or produce an emotion. Only thoughts that are of a personal nature affect an individual in a positive or negative way. These thoughts stimulate a feeling of some sort.

In his book *The Psychology of Emotions, Feelings and Thoughts,* Mark Pettinelli states, "emotions and feelings, although similar, have slight differences. They both are like conscious thought. However, emotions are closer to conscious thought. Feelings are defined as immediate unconscious thought. Feelings are faster than emotions. Feelings are sensations. Emotions are deeper than feelings."[1]

Emotions can be specifically labeled. Once we have a feeling and process it through conscious thought, we label it as an emotion. That is why after feeling a certain way and consciously considering it, we can describe the emotion as fear, joy, love, sadness, surprise, or anger.

Feelings change depending on the events that cause them. Emotions can become more defined if we continue to practice the thought that causes the feeling that produces the emotion. The emotion becomes part of our personality.

> *"Strong feelings*
> *energize*
> *our thoughts."*

The following are [2] definitions of the primary human emotions: *fear, joy, love, sadness, surprise* and *anger:*

Fear

Fear is a response to a dangerous situation that is about to happen, whether real or imagined. It is a human survival mechanism that triggers "fight or flight" to a negative stimulus. Fear can range from a slight cautionary thought to extreme phobia.

Joy

Joy or happiness is a state of mind responding to elements of enjoyment, satisfaction, and pleasure. It is accompanied by a sense of wellbeing, inner peace, love, safety, and contentment. Positive thinking and positive activities are characteristics of joy.

Love

Love arises from a feeling of profound oneness. Love can be platonic, romantic, religious, or familial. There are certain and subtle differences or distinctions in expressions of love regarding bonding, friendship, altruism, and philanthropy. Psychology suggests that love is to lend self-esteem to another.

Sadness

Sadness is associated with feelings of loss and disadvantage. A state of depression can result when a person consistently and intensely holds on to these feelings. Sloping body form, pouting and a lowered head along with reduced energy, quieted manner and withdrawal are all indicators of a depressive state.

Surprise

Unexpected events or results induce surprise. It is commonly accompanied by raised eyebrows, but also with horizontal lines on the forehead, a gaping mouth or jaw dropping, stretched skin below the eyebrows and wide, open eyelids.

Anger

Anger is evoked due to injustice, conflict, humiliation, negligence, or betrayal. Active anger can result in verbal or physical attack. If the anger is passive, the person internalizes these feelings by silently sulking. Tension and hostility are usually kept to oneself. Often, when one empathizes with another, anger may be displayed.

> *"Feelings can become part of our makeup."*

Strong feelings energize our thoughts

A thought with passion will certainly put those thoughts into motion. When we think and feel thoughts deep in our hearts, they become alive. The heart is the seat of our emotions. It is the feeling associated with a thought that energizes that thought.

When we speak of our emotions, we usually say we can feel them somewhere in our mid-section. "I felt butterflies in my stomach when they entered the room; it must be love." "What you said really hurt me to my heart" (extreme sadness). "The sudden news about the death of my close friend was gut wrenching" (sudden surprise).

We usually do not refer to feelings or emotions being felt in our heads, the seat of our intellect. That is where we think reasonable, logical thoughts. But what we think, when coupled with feelings and emotions from our 'heart,' is powerful, effective, and felt deep within.

"For as he thinketh in his heart, (with strong emotion) so is he" (Proverbs 23:7 KJV). You are what you think (in your heart). With heartfelt passion, you can fulfill your purpose in life. You will not live on purpose if you think halfheartedly. If you believe (rational, intention thought) in your heart, you can do most anything.

Feelings can become part of our makeup

Emotions are not always evenly distributed within each of us. There are people more balanced emotionally than others. Everyone knows someone who has an emotion that is more dominant and easier to identify. While some shows fear more often, others demonstrate love. Others are easily surprised, while few always are angry at something or someone. Some people have an abundance of joy, while others are sad beyond measure. Thoughts play a significant role in the causation of those dominant emotions.

People who are fearful (full of fear) are affected by the negative thoughts they have that eventually cause the emotion fear to become a part of their personality. They entertain thoughts that lend themselves to frightening endings, horrible outcomes, and scary situations for so long until they fear everything! This type of fear can lead to paranoia, intense fear or suspicion, or the feeling that something or someone is after them, when there is no apparent condition present.

Thoughts of fear may originate from a traumatic event during their first few precious years of life. Later in life, long after the memory of their childhood has gone into their subconscious, something triggers that "feeling" of that past event. The threat of unemployment, financial crisis or an unfamiliar noise while driving can all cause feelings of fear or impending doom.

Sometimes it arises when others get too close. They are on the brink of a wonderful partnership, a successful career or fulfilling their divine purpose, yet find a way to destroy that loving relationship to protect themselves from becoming "dangerously" close. They manage to "mess up" the opportunity to succeed or talk themselves out of following through on the idea that came to them seemingly "out of the blue."

> *"Feelings are faster*
> *than emotions."*

"I feel like something is about to happen." An emotional sensation takes over and produces negative thoughts that replay the feeling of the past. Something inside grips the mind until it becomes a fear-producing machine. Eventually, they become a fearful person; too paralyzed to accept any positive suggestions or affirmations.

We are not created to fear. It is impossible to fulfill your God-given purpose with fear ever present. Fear will cause a person to shrink back into a safe cave or assume a less challenging life until the perceived threat of imminent danger has passed.

2 Timothy 1:7 reads: *"For God has not given us a spirit of fear and timidity, but of power, love, and self-discipline." "For God did not give us a spirit of timidity (of cowardice, of craven and cringing and fawning fear), but [He has given us a spirit] of power and of love and of calm and well-balanced mind and discipline and self-control."* (Amplified Bible)

People are joyful (full of joy), not because of any event that causes pleasure or inner peace now, but because that feeling of happiness had been reinforced often enough and early enough that it has become the dominant emotion in their life.

Somewhere in their past, they experienced the feeling of a sense of wellbeing, inner peace, love, safety, and contentment. Maybe having the security of an attentive mother produced those feelings or their environment was filled with peace and comfort. Warm bottles, lullabies, frequent hugs, and kisses are expressions of love that can cause an infant to giggle joyfully.

Later in life, because they were admittedly "addicted" to warm, fuzzy feelings, their thoughts could not be anything less than wonderful and positive. No situation in life could force them to think deep down inside anything other than "everything is going to be alright."

When news of layoffs hits them, instead of fear, they feel secure that all will be well. They seem to fare well when life turns ugly. This is not to suggest they show no signs of concern about adverse things that happen in their life, but overall, their thoughts are positive and hopeful in nature.

These are the people who appear fearless and confident in the face of the most discouraging situations. In childhood, they were the children who laughed instead of crying their eyes out when the scoop of ice cream fell from the cone, knowing their parents will soon get them another one.

They always think positive thoughts no matter what the situation appears to be. When life gives them lemons, not only do they make lemonade, but they open a lemonade stand and sell it! They consider every setback a set-up for success; it is another opportunity to find and fulfill their purpose in life.

They will try anything once, attempting to dare but not foolish exploits. They go out on a limb in relationships, business, and adventures in life. Failure is viewed as another chance to succeed, and fear is an indication they need to get a little closer to the Creator for protection and comfort.

> *"For God has not given us a spirit of fear, but of power, love, and self-discipline."*

They have no more talent or abilities, (and sometimes less) than the fearful person. They have more exposure to conditions that lead to positive thoughts fueled by a sense of wellbeing, inner peace, love, safety, and contentment.

"And the peace of God, which transcends all understanding, will guard your hearts and your minds in Christ Jesus." –Philippians 4:7

Reviewing emotions that are a result of feelings and thoughts may help us understand why we act the way we do at times.

Our feelings toward our present situation may in fact be delayed reactions or repeated responses to what we have felt in the past under similar conditions. We may remain in "neutral," seeing little progress, until we learn to control our emotions and get a sense of our feelings.

Understand your feelings and emotions

We need to contact our feelings. Feeling stupid might make you feel bad only because your consistent thoughts of "I am stupid" unconsciously produces the bad feeling. Your focus is on "being stupid." Being in touch with our feelings can tell us why we have certain thoughts, especially the ones that detract us from our purpose.

Feelings and emotions make us aware that attention should be given to a thought, person, event, or experience related to that feeling. It should not be dismissed as trivial or insignificant. When we understand our feelings better, we can then use them in a more positive way. Recognize them and use them; just do not ignore them.

"I'm mad as hell and I'm not going to take it anymore." This famous quote from the movie "Network" demonstrates the results of expressed emotions. Howard Beale (actor Peter Finch) set off a series of events with his angry tirade, bringing about awareness and enlightenment to his society. Emotions, when properly expressed, can have unpredictable and remarkable results.

Our Creator gave us emotions so we can know where we are in relationship to life's events. Our emotions give us indicators that something is prompting us to experience fear, joy, love, sadness, surprise, or anger. These emotions can either serve our purpose toward or set us back from fulfilling our purpose.

> *"Being in touch with our feelings can tell us why we have certain thoughts."*

Fear can serve as an indicator that something can be both challenging and potentially dangerous. The fear may indicate our unwillingness to face changes or challenging times ahead in our lives. It is not necessarily a call to turn and run, but to press on knowing we need more encouragement, direction, or help. The fear can serve to heighten our awareness of the support around us and to accept that support when it comes.

The same can be applied not only to fear, but also to joy, love, sadness, surprise, and anger. Recognize, accept, and embrace these emotions, but do not be consumed nor controlled by them.

Do not allow emotions to get in the way of your efforts to accomplish your goals in life. We can become so joyful that we are oblivious to dangerous situations. We can love so much that we cannot let go of those things we need to let go of. We can become depressed with great sadness or in awe of and surprised by life's events to the point of stagnation. Not to mention, our out-of-control anger may even cause us to be next in line for serious jail time.

Feelings are to be used to accomplish our purpose in life, not to become overwhelmed by them. Nothing in life goes smoothly all the time. We need to be aware, by way of our feelings that things have become noticeably off key. Like a tuning fork to a piano, our feelings let us know when we are "out of tune" with our purpose.

Unfortunately, we concentrate more on the cause of the feelings and not the cure. We know something or someone has caused us to be off point and we focus on that instead of using our emotions to propel us toward our goal. Concentrate on feeling joy instead!

Embark on Deborah's journey as she evolves from sabotage to self-discovery.

Can she conquer the tumult of her emotions? Explore further...

Feelings Under Control?

In the bustling city of Collingwood, where aspirations clashed with emotions, there lived a young woman named Deborah. She was a paradox of emotions - intelligent yet impulsive, stunningly attractive yet emotionally turbulent. Anger, fear, and sadness were the constant companions, leaving her life unpredictable.

"Deborah, you cannot keep bottling up your feelings like this. It is not healthy," her friend Beckie remarked one evening as they sat in a cozy cafe, sipping hot lattes. Deborah sighed, her eyes reflecting a whirlwind of emotions.

"I just cannot help it, Bee. My feelings burst out of me like a dam breaking, flooding everything in their path." Beckie nodded in understanding, knowing too well the storm that brewed within Deborah's heart. Being in her mid-twenties, Deborah had a knack for starting relationships but a more severe habit of sabotaging them with her emotional outbursts. Her emotional roller coaster not only affected her personal life but also spilled over into her professional endeavors.

"Why do you let your emotions sabotage your success, Deb?" her colleague Jason once questioned, frustration evident in his voice. Deborah's brow creased, her mind replaying the countless times her feelings had clouded her judgment, leading to impulsive decisions, and missed opportunities. Instead of channeling her emotions towards constructive actions, she let them dictate her responses, often to her detriment.

One sunny afternoon, in the heart of her workplace, an incident unfolded that would serve as a tipping point in Deborah's tumultuous journey. A minor disagreement escalated into an intense argument, with Deborah's anger boiling over like a cauldron on fire. The aftermath was swift - trips to the manager's office, stern warnings, and eventually, a suspension that shattered her professional facade. Dejected and disillusioned, Deborah found herself teetering on the height of despair.

Rather than acknowledging the need to rein in her emotions, she spiraled into a whirlwind of sadness and self-doubt, retreating into a shell that shielded her from the world. Amidst the darkness that threatened to consume her, a glimmer of hope appeared in the form of her manager, Mr. Thompson – a man whose discerning gaze saw beyond the veneer of beauty to the depths of emotional turmoil within Deborah.

"Deborah, I believe in your potential, but you need to confront the demons of your past that haunt your present," Mr. Thompson spoke, his tone gentle yet firm. "Therapy is not an option; it is a necessity. And the company will cover the expenses." Reluctantly, Deborah embarked on a therapeutic journey that unearthed layers of childhood traumas buried beneath the sands of time. The wounds of abandonment, neglect, and loss cast long shadows on her adult life, shaping her emotional responses in ways she had never fathomed.

Through tear-stained sessions and heart-wrenching revelations, Deborah began to unravel the tangled web of her emotions, slowly untangling the knots that bound her. It was a journey of self-discovery, of facing fears long suppressed, and of embracing vulnerability as a strength rather than a weakness.

As the days turned into months, a transformation blossomed within Deborah's soul. The tempest that once raged uncontrollably now ebbed and flowed under her command, guided by newfound insights and emotional awareness. With a newfound sense of balance, Deborah returned to her workplace, carrying herself with a poise that commanded respect. Her job performance soared, catching the eye of the higher-ups who recognized her growth and dedication.

In an unexpected twist of fate, Deborah found herself forging not just professional connections, but personal bonds imbued with trust and authenticity. The walls she had built around her heart crumbled, paving the way for genuine relationships to bloom.

One sunny morning, as the rays of dawn painted the sky in hues of hope, Deborah stood at the threshold of a new beginning. The promotion to a management position was not just a symbol of her professional prowess but a testament to her resilience and reinvention.

"It is not about controlling your emotions, Deb. It is about embracing them, understanding them, and using them as fuel to propel you forward," her therapist's words echoed in her mind, a refrain of empowerment that she carried with her.

And so, Deborah - once a prisoner of her own feelings - emerged as a victor, her heart no longer a battleground but a sanctuary of acceptance and growth. She owed her transformation not to suppression but to expression, not to failure but to resilience, and not to fear but to courage. In the tapestry of life, Deborah's story intertwined with threads of vulnerability, strength, and redemption – is a testament to the power of gaining control over one's feelings for a more positive outcome.

"I feel that something is happening!"

Chapter 3

Speak

Speak [1]

- to utter words or articulate sounds with ordinary speech modulation; talk.

- to convey thoughts, opinions, or emotions orally.

- to make a statement in writing: "The biography speaks of great loneliness."

- to convey a message by nonverbal means: "Actions speak louder than words."

- to make a reservation or request. Often used with for: "I spoke for the last slice of pizza."

"What are you saying?"

Say what you mean and mean what you say. Does this sound familiar? But how many of us consider this important message either very lightly or not at all. We constantly throw words around as if they are meaningless. Some use coarse jesting, which can cause severe damage to the person who is the butt of their jokes. Others make frivolous promises that leave people wanting, waiting and gravely disappointed.

Some have shaped the lives of others, positively or negatively, by the very words they speak to them. Still others have "self-talked" their way out of great opportunities, prosperity, wellbeing or fulfilling their divine purpose in life. Words are immensely powerful.

Words are more powerful than thoughts

"I know what you are thinking!" How many times have we felt that and was absolutely correct? It happens more often than we consider. How is that possible? Thoughts project feelings. Sometimes you may feel what another person is thinking. Somehow, those thoughts are so passionate they fill the room and you can feel it.

But words expressed verbally are more powerful than thoughts. Spoken words are exact. You know clearly and precisely what someone is saying. If there is a question about what one has said, there may be opportunity for clarity. We can process words and consider what we say before we say it. When we learn to think and feel on purpose, then our spoken words will become more intentional and effective.

> *"Words are more powerful than thoughts."*

But unfortunately, sometimes we are not careful with our words. We offer thoughtless words toward serious issues in life. We carelessly comment on things that we have little, or even worse, unclear information about. More often than not, our hasty speech comes back to bite us where it hurts the most – not in our posterior, but rather in our purpose. It's difficult to fulfill your purpose in life when you are using words that have negative impact. Words are very powerful and creative.

Many relationships have ended, deals have "gone south" and even lives have been destroyed because words were spoken in haste. Emotional words spoken with passion energizes and quickly activates a thought. Words influence situations and circumstances greater than thoughts can.

Words create

All words come from a single thought. We think and then we speak. This includes words we do not mean and words we speak in jest. A "thoughtless word" is actually a word spoken without consideration, but not without thought. We think a thought and express it in words. These words become active the minute we speak them.

Deep inside we know this is true. That is why after someone says something that has potentially adverse effects, such as, "I wish they would just drop dead," a natural response would be: "Please don't put that out there" or "Don't say that!" We actually fear sudden death could happen.

> *"Sticks and stones may break my bones, but words will never hurt me"*

Words are creative. They produce, in an unexplainable way, what they mean. "I just know I'm going to get sick," strangely enough find you suffering from a cold or fever the next day. "I always get the job I want," have kept you employed and successfully advancing in your career. It is not that mysterious, but it does require that you really believe in your heart what you say.

Let us not think that things will not happen if we do not speak them into existence. They do. If you never utter a word, you will still be unable to avoid the issues of life. However, when we do speak positively, we keep things going and speed them along in the right direction.

Words were used to begin man's physical history. In the beginning God said, "Let there be light," and there was light. God spoke all creation into existence and enjoyed it! He stepped back from His work, took note and saw that it was good.

God used words, not mere thoughts, to create the universe and everything in it. He used words to create us in His image and gave us the ability to use words to create. We too, should look back at the great positive effects our words have in our own world around us. We should enjoy speaking greatness into our children's lives, peace and security into our home life, and success and fulfillment into our own lives.

Words can hurt

The popular saying, "sticks and stones may break my bones, but words will never hurt me" is a gross misconception. Words not only hurt, but sometimes they cause severe pain and agony, to the point of death. There have been a growing number of suicides reported that were caused by the pain of harsh words. Countless lives have been permanently altered because of unkind words spoken by someone close to them.

Some children have had a multitude of discouraging words spoken to them during their formative years and live out those words the rest of their lives. Labels have been placed on them that are nothing short of verbal abuse, such as nicknames degrading their physical appearance. Names tagging them as fat and ugly, or poking fun at the size of their nose, hairstyle, walk, speech, and other personal traits not easily changed are doled out on a regular basis.

Friends and co-workers can also be cruel without knowing the damage their joking can do. We call it "just busting your chops," when in reality, we are berating and beating down that person. "What are you, stupid?" "You big dummy." "Is that the best you can do?" "It's a good thing yo' momma died at childbirth; if she hada' seent you, she woulda' died of shame."

Horrible, hurtful words are often intended to be taken in stride as part of some sort of cultural rite of passage. This type of socially accepted "ribbing" usually ends in, "I was just kidding." But the words spoken do not end there. They continue to do their work within the person receiving the clever, cutting phrases.

Worst of all is our self-talk. We speak words about ourselves that do more damage than we imagine. "I'm sooo fat!" "I am so stupid." "I guess they were right; I'll never make it." "I can't do this by myself." "I'll never be able to accomplish anything." Self-talk can be more damaging than what others say because we are always with ourselves. We hardly ever take a break from speaking words to ourselves that focus on our shortcomings and failures.

In the short run, negative words spoken about a person can sting. Eventually, they can do permanent, irrevocable damage. Sadly, although mostly unintentionally, the harshest words often come from people we know and love.

Words can heal

As badly as words may hurt, they can also heal. There is nothing quite as soothing as a compliment. "You look good today." "I'm so glad to see you." "I hope you have a great day!" "You are a beautiful person."

> "The words you say will either *acquit* you or *condemn* you."

Words have healing power. Words have the power to go out into the air and do what they are designed to do. When we say healing words, whether in the presence of the person in need or just out in the atmosphere, the results are remarkably the same. That is why we pray for those who are sick. There is an example of this in Matthew 8:5:

"When Jesus returned to Capernaum, a Roman officer came and pleaded with him, "Lord, my young servant lies in bed, paralyzed and in terrible pain." Jesus said, "I will come and heal him."

But the officer said, "Lord, I am not worthy to have you come into my home. Just say the word from where you are, and my servant will be healed. I know this because I am under the authority of my superior officers, and I have authority over my soldiers. I only need to say, 'Go,' and they go, or 'Come,' and they come. And if I say to my slaves, 'Do this,' they do it." When Jesus heard this, he was amazed.

Then Jesus said to the Roman officer, "Go back home. Because you believed, it has happened." And the young servant was healed that same hour."

We should learn to use our words more for soothing and less for scorning, for more healing and less hurting. Instead of bashing people with harsh words, let us begin basking people with warm, soothing words. Guys, I know this may not sound macho, but it just might improve our environment, particularly our relationships.

Everyone needs and deserves a "verbal massage" every now and then. What we get many times is a "tongue lashing" instead. Let us face it, the world is getting more difficult to deal with day by day. People are enduring elevated levels of stress at home, on the job, in school and on the way to and from wherever they are traveling. No one wants to give anyone a break. Long gone are the days of that great American classic by John A. Lomax (1910):

"Home, home on the range,
Where the deer and the antelope play.
Where seldom is heard a discouraging word
And the skies are not cloudy all day."[1]

Now, consider the last verse of the 1973 hit by Stevie Wonder, "Living for the City":

"I hope you hear inside my voice of sorrow
And that it motivates you to make a better tomorrow
This place is cruel nowhere could be much colder

If we do not change the world will soon be over
Living just enough, just enough for the city!"[2]

We can change the world through our use of words. Words can heal, but we must speak them with conviction. We must be dedicated to starting with ourselves. Speak positive, motivating words to ourselves, then to those closest to us and finally to those we meet along the way.

"You are the salt of the earth. But what good is salt if it has lost its flavor? Can you make it salty again? It will be thrown out and trampled underfoot as worthless." –Matthew 5:13

Salt preserves and adds flavor wherever it finds itself. Our words may be the only salt someone receives at the very moment they need it. We are here to help, heal and preserve life whenever possible. It does not cost us anything to speak a kind word, but there is a price to pay if we hold back. If we who are salt refuse to "shake," the world would be a little more "tasteless."

Practicing speaking words that heal rather than hurt will move us closer to fulfilling our purpose in life. We will become more sensitive to the feelings and needs of others. We will be able to speak words that are more genuine and believable.

Words with feelings are enormously powerful

Words accompanied by emotions and feelings are enormously powerful. To be able to feel what someone is saying is quite effective. It is a matter of fact that people use their emotions, and not necessarily their logic, to receive what a speaker says and to judge whether it is true. This is why we must be enthusiastic about what we are saying in order to be taken seriously. When a message is believed, people will then decide how they will respond to it.

If a person comes to your door, rings the bell and after opening the door you hear, "Are you Mr./Ms. Williams?" You inquisitively reply, "Yes, what is it?" The person then responds, completely void of emotion and in a low, flat voice, "You just won ten million dollars." You will look at that person in disbelief and say, "No thank you," and quickly close the door. You would then wonder what kind of fraud they were trying to get over on you.

> *"Words are much more*
> *powerful*
> *than you imagine."*

But what if that person at the door was the late Ed McMahon or a representative for American Family Sweepstakes excitedly announcing: "YOU JUST WON THE AMERICAN FAMILY SWEEPSTAKES!!!" You would jump up and down, do a few cartwheels, scream, or do whatever your body could stand because, not only did those words have emotion, but they became believable enough for such a response. Some winners of substantial amounts of money have even responded by fainting!

But to convince someone else, you must believe it and feel it yourself. Your words will indeed carry the emotion, or the feelings attached to them.

Be very aware of your emotions before you blurt out something you cannot take back.

Matthew 12:33 reads: *"A tree is identified by its fruit. If a tree is good, its fruit will be good. If a tree is bad, its fruit will be bad. For whatever is in your heart determines what you say.*

A good person produces good things from the treasury of a good heart, and an evil person produces evil things from the treasury of an evil heart. And I tell you this, you must give an account on judgment day for every idle word you speak. The words you say will either acquit you or condemn you."

Words will be formed out of your heart for either good or bad purposes. Be certain your heart is right before you speak. The place where your emotions are rooted, if gone unchecked, can either result in your condemnation or acquittal, not so much in the court of law, but in the court of life. As your emotions cause your tongue to be loose, you can speak words that will cause your life to move towards fulfilling its purpose or move it tragically away from its divine goal.

Words can cause life or death

Proverbs 18:21 reads, *"The tongue can bring death or life; those who love to talk will reap the consequences."*

There is no other way to say it except, be careful with your words. Words spoken in the heat of the moment often lead to regret. People have lost their entire fortunes because of what was said during an emotional outburst. We should not make promises or establish contracts when we are less logical and more emotional.

Genesis 25:29-34 tells of one who lost his God-given rights and privileges because of ill-spoken words.

"One day when Jacob was cooking some stew, Esau arrived home from the wilderness exhausted and hungry. Esau said to Jacob, "I am starved! Give me some of that red stew!" (This is how Esau got his other name, Edom, which means "red.") "All right," Jacob replied, "but trade me your rights as the firstborn son."

"Look, I'm dying of starvation!" said Esau. "What good is my birthright to me now?" But Jacob said, "First you must swear that your birthright is mine." So, Esau swore an oath, thereby selling all his rights as the firstborn to his brother, Jacob.

Then Jacob gave Esau some bread and lentil stew. Esau ate the meal, then got up and left. He showed contempt for his rights as the firstborn."

I am sure if Esau could take it back, he would have gladly gone hungry a few more hours than live with his belly full of regret for the rest of his life. For a few beans, he gave away the farm and all that his father Isaac had inherited from his father Abraham. Esau would now have to live as the second-born son instead of in his God-given role as firstborn.

This story may not have as much impact on us as our own failure to watch our words. Many have spoken careless words that have destroyed careers, marriages, families, and futures.

Some of us suffer needlessly because we cannot keep our mouths shut. If harboring a single thought for a fleeting period of time has the potential of creating other similar thoughts, I believe it is similar for words. Once we get on a roll, our tongue has a mind of its own. Whatever the subject is, positive or negative, once we talk past a certain point, it is impossible to stop. We will go on and on without a breath, and no one will get a word in edgewise. It is as if no one is there except the one who is talking.

Those longwinded soliloquies are not without consequences. If nothing more than a missed opportunity to hear someone else's story or opinion, it is damaging to a person to expend more than their share of words during a conversation. We will be held accountable for every idle word spoken.

"Even fools are thought wise when they keep silent; with their mouths shut, they seem intelligent" (Proverbs 17:28). It pays to be more eager to listen than to speak. We could hear other perspectives and opinions as well as valuable wisdom, especially from those who have traveled this way long before us. It would also prevent us from waxing eloquently with our own foolishness.

As the older generation would say, *"Speak when spoken to; children should be seen and not heard."* Perhaps they were right. We would be wise to listen.

Observe the impact of Diana's thoughtless words on her life; they truly wield significant power. Delve deeper into her story...

Watch Your Words

Diana stood at her kitchen counter, her fingers tapping restlessly against the cool marble surface. The room was filled with the quiet hum of the refrigerator, the only sound in an otherwise silent apartment. She glanced at her reflection in the window above the sink, the lines of her face seeming more pronounced than ever.

Forty-four years old, and what did she have to show for it? Three failed relationships, no children, and a string of business ventures that never quite took off.

"Diana, you really need to lighten up," Barbara's voice echoed in her mind. Her best friend had always been her sounding board, her voice of reason. "You've got to be careful with your words. They have a way of coming back to bite you."

Diana sighed, reaching for her coffee cup. The truth was, she had a habit of speaking her mind, often without thinking. It was a trait that had driven more than one man away, including Gerald. Gerald, with his easy smile and patient demeanor, had been her last chance at a meaningful relationship. But her constant critical chatter had worn him down, until one day he simply walked away.

"Remember Gerald?" Barbara had reminded her during one of their many heart-to-heart conversations. "He slipped out of your life because you couldn't stop criticizing him. You never saw the good in him, only the flaws."

Diana took a sip of her coffee, the bitter taste mirroring her mood. She had always prided herself on being honest, but honesty had become a weapon rather than a virtue. She had wielded her words carelessly, cutting down the people who had dared to get close to her.

And it was not just her personal life that had suffered. Her business ventures had followed a similar pattern. She had started each one with enthusiasm, but her pessimistic outlook had quickly overshadowed any potential for success. "It'll never work," she had muttered more times than she could count. "This is doomed to fail." And, as if her words held some kind of dark magic, fail they did.

Barbara's advice had always been the same. "Diana, you need to change your mindset. Start seeing and speaking about success instead of failure. Words are much more powerful than you imagine."

But changing a lifetime of negative thinking was easier said than done. Diana knew that better than anyone. She set her coffee cup down and picked up her phone, scrolling through her contacts until she found Barbara's number. Maybe talking to her best friend would help clear her head.

"Hey, Barb," Diana said when Barbara answered. "Got a minute?"

"For you, always," Barbara replied. "What's on your mind?"

"I've been thinking about what you said. About my words, and how they've... sabotaged things."

Barbara was silent for a moment. "It's not easy to hear, but I'm glad you're thinking about it. You know, our words shape our reality. If you keep expecting the worst, that's exactly what you'll get."

Diana felt a lump form in her throat. "I just don't know how to stop. It's like, as soon as I start to hope for something good, this voice in my head tells me it's not going to happen."

"That's the negativity talking," Barbara said gently. "You have to fight it. Challenge those thoughts. When you catch yourself being critical or pessimistic, try to turn it around. It won't be easy, but it's a start."

Diana nodded, even though Barbara could not see her. "I guess it's worth a shot. I don't want to keep losing people... or opportunities."

Barbara's voice softened. "You've got so much potential, Diana. I have always believed that. But you have to believe it too. And you have to start speaking like you believe it."

After their call ended, Diana sat in her quiet apartment, thinking about Barbara's words. Could it really be that simple? Could changing her words change her life? She was not sure, but she knew one thing: she could not keep going the way she had been. Something had to give.

Over the next few weeks, Diana made a conscious effort to change her internal dialogue. When she caught herself thinking something negative, she forced herself to find a positive counterpoint. It was exhausting, and more often than not, she felt like she was fighting a losing battle. But she kept at it, determined to see if Barbara was right.

One evening, as she was going through some old paperwork, she found a business proposal she had abandoned months ago. It was an idea she had been enthusiastic about, but her doubts had convinced her it would never work. She read through it again, and for the first time, allowed herself to imagine it succeeding.

"This could work," she said aloud, assessing the words on her tongue. "This might actually work."

A small, hesitant smile tugged at the corners of her mouth. Just maybe, there was a chance.

Weeks turned into months, and Diana found herself slipping back into old habits. The fight against her negativity was a constant struggle, and she was not always successful. Her business proposal remained just that—a proposal, collecting dust on her desk. She still found it hard to believe in herself, and her relationships with others continued to suffer.

One night, after yet another argument with a colleague, Diana called Barbara in tears. "I'm trying, Barb, I really am. But it is so hard. I feel like I'm not getting anywhere."

Barbara listened patiently before speaking. "Change is never easy, Diana. And it does not happen overnight. But every little step you take is progress. Don't give up on yourself."

Diana wiped her tears away. "I just wish I could see some results. It feels like I'm stuck in the same place, no matter what I do."

Barbara's voice was firm but kind. "Remember what I told you about words? You have to keep speaking positively, even when it is hard. Especially when it's hard."

Despite Barbara's encouragement, Diana's resolve began to waver. She started to doubt whether she could ever change. Her critical nature seemed too deeply ingrained, her negative words too powerful to overcome. She found herself slipping back into old patterns, her hope fading with each passing day.

One evening, as she sat alone in her apartment, Diana received an e-mail from a potential investor who had shown interest in her business proposal. Her heart raced as she read the message, her mind filling with a mixture of excitement and dread. This could be the opportunity she had been waiting for, the chance to finally prove herself. But as she sat down to draft a response, the familiar voice of doubt crept in.

"They're not really interested," she muttered to herself. "They'll back out once they see your plan."

She stared at the screen, her fingers hovering over the keyboard. The weight of her own negativity felt crushing, paralyzing her with fear. She wanted to believe in the possibility of success, but her own words held her back, casting a dark shadow over her aspirations.

In the end, Diana's response to the investor was lukewarm, her enthusiasm tempered by her doubts. The opportunity slipped through her fingers, just as so many others had before. She watched helplessly as her dreams faded, her own words sealing her fate.

Barbara's words echoed in her mind, a painful reminder of the power she had squandered. "Words are much more powerful than you imagine." Diana had learned that lesson the hard way, her own negativity sabotaging her life goals, her relationships, and her happiness.

In the quiet of her apartment, Diana realized the devastating effects of her own self-sabotage. She had spoken her mind, but in doing so, she had spoken herself into a life of loneliness and unfulfilled potential. Her words, once a source of pride, had become her greatest enemy, a constant reminder of what she had lost.

And so, Diana continued on, her life a testament to the destructive power of negative words. She had tried to change, but in the end, she had been unable to escape the shadow of her own doubts and criticisms. Her story was a cautionary tale, a reminder of the importance of words and the power they held over our lives. Without a happy ending, Diana's life stood as a stark warning of the consequences of unchecked negativity, a legacy of missed opportunities and unfulfilled dreams.

"What are you saying?"

THINK FEEL SPEAK WRITE- DO

Chapter 4

Write

Write [1]

- to trace or form (characters, letters, words, etc.) on the surface of some material, as with a pen, pencil, or other instrument or means.

- to express or communicate in writing; give a written account of.

- to compose and produce in words or characters duly set down; to write a letter to a friend.

- to produce as author or composer; to write a sonnet or a symphony.

- to cause to be apparent or unmistakable: "Honesty is written on his face."

"Write it down."

L
ike many of you, I have a problem remembering day to day things I have to do. I have tried all types of methods to improve my memory, from herbal solutions to technical devices. After a few mini victories and many failed attempts, I stumbled on a solution that surpasses any modern technical method – a pad and a pen.

Writing things down is a tried-and-true method of remembering anything, from names and phone numbers to grocery items, appointments and other various "things to do." Where electronic recording devices may fail when damaged, malfunctioning or exert difficulty in learning to use, a pen or pencil to paper always works.

But writing serves an even higher purpose than merely listing agendas or common things to remember. Writing is incredibly significant in fulfilling one's purpose in life.

Habakkuk 2:2 reads: *"And the Lord answered me and said, Write the vision and engrave it so plainly upon tablets that everyone who passes may [be able to] read [it easily and quickly] as he hastens by."* (Amplified Bible)

We are encouraged to write things down that are of a higher order. These are things that pertain to what we think, what we imagine and what we see for our future or our very purpose in life.

We are exhorted to make it permanent and plain, not only for later reference but so that others may be informed as to our intentions and aspirations. Who knows? They will be significant in assisting us in fulfilling our purpose.

Writing clarifies your vision

In order to clearly write what you envision doing or where you are going in life that others may understand, it must be clear to you the road on which you are traveling. You must know for certain what your vision is and that your mind is made up. To convince others to "run" with your vision, you must first convince yourself. Writing these things down helps tremendously.

Why is it so important to know your purpose in life? We may not realize the awful consequences that not knowing one's true purpose may cause, but many medical conditions and relationship problems can be attributed to people not knowing their God-given assignment.

All forms of addictions, abuses, extreme materialism, depression, and other emotional issues could be a result of a person's attempt to silence the unceasing call of their own destiny heard in their mind and felt in their spirit. We cannot truly have peace until we put all the pieces of our lives together.

Knowing your purpose enables you to have a center point of focus to which other things take a back seat. There is much truth to the popular saying, "Idle hands are the devil's workshop." This means that if you have little or no idea of what to do, you will find yourself doing things that are not in line with your divine purpose. You will engage in 'busywork' or mindless entertainment rather than moving forward down your preordained life's path.

> *"Writing forces us to state facts, not fiction."*

When you write things down, you tend to give them more thought than if you only spoke them. The writing thought process is more intense and exact. You must choose your words and put sentences together in a way that is easily read and understood. You have the opportunity to erase, rearrange, rewrite, or start over entirely, which often you cannot do with the spoken word.

You can read over your written text and have others read it as well. You have tools available at your disposal to ensure its accuracy and validity. You can use an electronic spell checker and/or thesaurus or an old-fashioned dictionary. All these tools are available to assist you in putting your thoughts on paper in the best way possible.

Begin to write your own thoughts concerning your vision or purpose. For some of you, this may be the first time doing this. To get started, answer the following questions: What do you think you should be doing in the near future? What do you like to do presently? What did you enjoy or not enjoy doing in your past? What are you doing now that is truly fulfilling?

Spend valuable time writing the answers to these questions. Soon, you will experience the exhilaration of your creative juices beginning to flow. The more you focus on writing, the clearer your vision will become. The clearer it is to you, the more comprehensible it will be for others.

The results are invaluable. You will suddenly feel alive again. You will begin to get excited over your discovery and will want to share the experience with others. Proverbs 29:18 states:

"Where there is no vision [no redemptive revelation of God], the people perish; but he who keeps the law [of God, which includes that of man]—blessed (happy, fortunate, and enviable) is he." (Amplified Bible)

A vision for a person's life does wonders, not only for the recipient but also for those around them who will benefit from the fulfilled vision. Pursuing and performing one's purpose has far-reaching results.

Writing invites others to respond

Personal thoughts are sometimes considered to be intimate and private in nature. It is immensely difficult, although possible, to know one's thoughts until they are shared through written or spoken words. When a person does open up to expose their secret thoughts to another, they often may want it to remain between the two.

> "Our vision should *beg* for others to *share* in it."

However, when these thoughts are written down for all to see, it begs for a response of some sort. It no longer holds the same meaning as a private thought shared in close quarters. It becomes an advertisement of sorts, waiting for a reaction or retort by those viewing it. The message can be viewed again and again until it is burned into a person's psyche.

That is why billboards are so effective. No matter how fast you drive by the message is so clearly stated and the image so striking that when seen, it both grabs your attention and invokes a response. Habakkuk 2:2 says: *"Then the Lord said to me, "Write my answer plainly on tablets, so that a runner can carry the correct message to others. This vision is for a future time. It describes the end, and it will be fulfilled. If it seems slow in coming, wait patiently, for it will surely take place. It will not be delayed."*

Habakkuk, the prophet of God, was instructed to write the answer to his provocative questions in such a way that others could respond. He was instructed how to cover all bases including durability, clarity, and accuracy. In the case of perceived delays, the fulfillment of the message would still be believable, and people are encouraged to wait for it.

Our writings concerning our purpose should be cautiously shared with others. We should be aware of the care we need to take to ensure our message is rational, moving, and trustworthy. Our vision should beg for others to share in it. No one can be hugely successful if he alone participates in and benefits from his ideas.

When an individual or company has a vision for a business, in order to get financial support from other individuals or organizations, a written business plan is often required. It must be clear, and the vision must be well thought of by the supportive cast. Many ventures have stalled in the beginning phase because of a lack of support. What they actually lacked was a convincing vision statement.

Your purpose in life is waiting for a chance to shine among the masses. Since our Creator is the source of all productive and positive thoughts, imaginations, and visions, it is reasonable to believe His purpose is to see to completion what He has given us. He is a willing participant in our vision. In other words, He is "pro" the vision He has given and will give provision to complete it.

But the process of due diligence on our part cannot be overlooked. That is, steps must be taken by those of us with the vision to ensure the idea is worthy of completion. After close inspection, or more appropriately, introspection, looking within ourselves, checking our motives, inner thoughts and desires, our findings must be concluded as healthy, viable and moral before others will begin to draw close to the fantastic vision we have.

Pray as much as you would like, but unless you have done all you can do, after praying, to be completely honest with yourself concerning your shortcomings, it will be difficult to move toward fulfilling your purpose. Write down those things that are weighing you down, robbing you of your focus, preventing you from moving toward your goal or hindering your progression.

Also, write down those negative thoughts that hold your divine purpose hostage in the prison of your mind. Seek to expose, eliminate, discard, and destroy even the smallest sign of negative roadblocks to you fulfilling your purpose. Paul also encourages us in Hebrews 12:1 with these words:

"Therefore, since we are surrounded by such a huge crowd of witnesses to the life of faith, let us strip off every weight that slows us down, especially the sin that so easily trips us up. And let us run with endurance the race God has set before us."

Be certain you are not playing the "blame game" by identifying circumstances and people you feel have gotten in your way. What is bad about painful, disappointing experiences is not learning from them. Write down your personal issues, things that you take ownership of, and get rid of them. Observe closely your attitude about the people in your life and the situations you have allowed to overrun or limit your movement toward your goal.

Writing helps to clear your path on purpose

When you write your personal thoughts, especially as they relate to your vision and purpose, you have the opportunity to see where you are going and just as importantly, where you have come from. It is impossible to move forward unless you know where you have been. Knowing your past is crucial to fulfilling your purpose so that you do not repeat the same mistakes or end up on the same dead-end road as before.

> *"Writing enables others to participate in your vision."*

As you pen your goals using whatever method you choose, you will start to see patterns of behavior that you may have never stopped to notice before. You may see where you got in your own way, or the influence others have had in your life experiences. You may see missed opportunities or snap decisions gone wrong. You may become aware of negative habits that you have.

When you continue to think with the intent to write, your mind will recall many incidents that may have plagued your life for years: The angry responses that end important relationships; those horrible, self-degrading thoughts that stop you cold in your tracks; that feeling of fear that arises each time you are reminded of a particular traumatic event will all come rushing back.

Dig deep into your past as you write. Own those things that caused you great pain, extreme joy, or tremendous challenge. Write how you responded to each. Jot down the list of your successful attempts at individual achievements as well as your miserable failures.

Be honest with yourself. Try not to exclude embarrassing moments since these are also part of your past. Remember, this is for you to fulfill your purpose in life. This is for your eyes only. Once you write, review periodically, celebrate your victories, mourn your losses, get rid of the negatives, and move on. Do not dwell on or live in the past. You must do the work now if you are to fulfill your purpose in life.

Next, define your present situation. Is it satisfying and healthy or unfulfilling and dysfunctional? Write what you are doing now. Explain in detail why you are doing whatever it is that occupies most of your time. Do not just think about it or talk about it, write it down.

Writing is a serious action. It forces you to face where you actually are in life without exaggeration. Writing forces us to state facts, not fiction. Unless you are completely satisfied that you are living out your purpose, doing what you were created to do in life, then you owe it to yourself to investigate further. Spend some time and energy doing this.

Circle the experiences you would love to repeat and cross out those you would never want to happen again. Write how each experience either helped or hindered the process of fulfilling your purpose. There were times you thought you were being treated unfairly, when actually it could have been a prompt to move forward or move toward your life's goal. Writing these things down helps you to gain clarity concerning your path.

When you have completed the introspection of your past and present life, with passion and excitement begin to write your future dreams, aspirations, and vision. Write as if there are no obstacles to reaching your goals. Write freely; you have nothing to lose and a whole new life with more purpose and focus to gain. That idea you have that will not go away. Write it down. That business or service you get so excited about every time you think about it. Write it down. The new skill you want to learn, classes you want to take, places you want to go and people you want to connect with – write all of it down!

Writing enables others to participate in your vision

When writing your vision and your purpose, write so that others may read it with crystal-clear understanding. As Habakkuk 2:2 states: *"So that a runner can carry the correct message to others."*

Many plans and purposes have been unwittingly sabotaged by others who were excited to participate but were running with the wrong message. Your purpose must be unmistakably clear.

But when others participate with the correct message, it is amazing what can be accomplished. Many successful men and women have credited their achievements to having one or more individuals who understood the mission, joined the cause, and made great strides on their behalf. Others have received phenomenal philanthropic financial support that ensured the fulfillment of a grandiose vision.

Believe it. When your vision message or stated purpose is clear, there are a host of supporters waiting to run with it.

Dexter Wells took great pride in his ability to eloquently articulate his ideas to others, yet he harbored a significant flaw—he adamantly refused to put his thoughts on paper. Read more..

Why write it down?

exter Wells, a middle-aged energetic man with a perpetual sparkle in his eye and a contagious enthusiasm, was known around town for his boundless creativity and innovative spirit. One day, Dexter had what he believed to be a ground breaking business idea that he was convinced would revolutionize the community.

He eagerly shared his vision with anyone who would lend an ear, from the local pastors like Reverend Weldon to his close friend Corey.

And even to strangers he struck up conversations with at the local coffee shop.

Dexter's excitement was noticeable as he painted vivid pictures with his words, describing how his idea would bring about positive change and growth for the town.

On day while at the local coffee shop, Dexter, sipping his coffee between an animated conversation with the barista, is approached by a stranger.

"Mind if I join you?", the stranger asked.

"Of course! Please, have a seat. I'm Dexter."

"Nice to meet you, Dexter. I couldn't help but overhear your enthusiastic conversation with the barista. What's on your mind?"

"Ah, just sharing my vision for the town. I truly believe we can create something special here, something that brings people together and spurs growth."

"That sounds intriguing. What's your vision for our town?"

With eyes lighting up, Dexter replies, "Imagine a community garden right in the heart of our town, where people can come together, grow their own produce, and share meals. It's a place for connection, sustainability, and a sense of belonging."

"That sounds wonderful, Dexter. How do you envision making this idea a reality?"

Dexter thoughtfully explained, "I've been reaching out to local businesses for support and gathering a group of volunteers to help with the planning and execution. It's a collective effort, and I believe we can achieve great things together."

"I admire your dedication and enthusiasm, Dexter. It's inspiring to see someone so enthusiastic about making a positive impact in our community. I would like to read more about your idea. I believe I may have a way to help make that happen."

Little did Dex know but the stranger was actually the executive director of a local foundation that was looking to fund projects similar to the one he had in mind, but sadly not on paper.

That was a critical flaw in Dexter's approach –he never took the time to write down his idea in a concrete and organized manner. "I'll get to it eventually," he would say, dismissing the importance of putting his thoughts on paper. "Just listen to what it's about for now."

As Dexter's enthusiasm continued to spread, his friend Jessica, a sharp and pragmatic business major from Temple University, grew increasingly concerned. She recognized the potential of Dexter's idea but also saw the glaring need for a structured business plan to turn that vision into reality.

"Dex, you need to put your idea on paper," Jessica urged him one day over coffee. "I can help you with that. Let's sit down and outline your business plan. The deadline for funding applications is approaching fast."

But Dexter, caught up in the whirlwind of his own excitement, kept postponing Jessica's offer, convinced that his charisma and passion alone would be enough to rally the support he needed. Opportunity after opportunity for financial and moral backing slipped through his fingers as he continued to neglect the advice of those who cared about him.

Days turned into weeks, and still, Dexter persisted in sharing his idea verbally without taking the crucial step of documenting it. Reverend Weldon gently reminded him of the wisdom in Habakkuk 2:2, emphasizing the importance of making the vision plain and accessible to others.

As the deadline for funding applications loomed ever closer, Jessica's frustration reached a boiling point. "Dex, you're letting this slip away," she admonished him firmly. "If only there were written materials - a website, a brochure, a business plan - something tangible for people to read and support. You're missing your chance to make a real difference."

In the end, despite Dexter's unwavering passion and the genuine interest of the community, his business idea never took off. The lack of a concrete plan and the failure to heed the advice of those offering to help proved to be insurmountable obstacles.

Dexter learned a valuable lesson the hard way – that a vision, no matter how brilliant, remains just a dream without the discipline and commitment to put it into words and actions. And as he reflected on what could have been, he knew that the words of Habakkuk would forever ring true in his mind:

"Write the vision, make it plain so that whoever passes by may easily read it and run with it."

"Write it down."

Chapter 5

Do [1]

- to execute; effect; perform (an act, action, etc.)

- to carry out; fulfill: "Do what I tell you."

- to bring to completion; finish.

- to bring about; cause; produce.

- to exert (efforts, etc.): "Do your best."

"Just do it!"

D on't just talk about it. ***Do it!*** Actions speak louder than thoughts, feelings, and words! Many of us often say, "I was just about to do that." We have good intentions, lofty ideas and often the ways and means to get things done. Yet, we sometimes fail at putting into action what we believe we should do.

Faith without works is dead. We say, "Do not doubt what God can do." We believe in His Omnipotence, His Omnipresence and His Omniscience. We believe He can do anything except fail. We know of His creative power to form something from nothing. God Rules!

But this call to "DO" is not directed toward our Creator; it is to those of us who have discovered our purpose in life. We are each given the ability to manifest what we have imagined or desired if it is in alignment with God's purpose for our lives. Unless we DO something with our thoughts, feelings, spoken and written words, we will not accomplish our purpose in life.

So, how do we put all of this into action? There is an uncomplicated process that requires significant effort on our part. No one else will do it for us. It is not easy, but it is achievable. It will take diligence and discipline, but the rewards far outweigh the difficulties you may encounter. Use this as a straightforward guide to assist you in fulfilling your purpose.

> ## "Think accurate thoughts."

As we have discovered, much like an automobile uses four tires to efficiently arrive at your designated destination, our divine purpose also has four "tires" or steps to reach our goal of fulfillment.

By thinking positively, having your feelings or emotions under control, speaking words that will promote rather than sabotage, and purposefully and concisely writing the idea or vision, the "doing" becomes automatically.

Think your way to fulfilling your purpose

We are now well aware of the power of thoughts. We know that thoughts can create conditions for success or failure, greatness, or mediocrity. But first you must have a powerful desire to know and fulfill your purpose in life. If you have a desire to be what God has created you to be, you must begin with your thoughts.

Think accurate thoughts.

"No matter what I do,
I can't get ahead or do enough."

"If I have all that I really want,
people will be jealous of me."

"No one loves me for myself."

"Everybody cannot be rich; there is not
enough money for everyone."

"It is what it is!"

When thoughts like these are dominant in our mind, they prevent us from moving toward the purpose for which we were created. We must admit that these thoughts are inaccurate. We can no longer accept them as true. No matter how long we have accepted these or other negative thoughts, or what evidence we have to prove their validity, it is simply wrong to think these thoughts.

How do we know when we are having negative thoughts? What can we rely on to give us warning that we are in danger of sinking our own ship?

Our feelings and emotions give us indication that something is wrong with our thinking. If you begin to feel negative as a result of a thought, then the thought is negative. That is not to say that you ignore the facts; just do not ignore the opposing positive thought as well.

If you feel sad, angry, helpless, hopeless, frustrated, or fearful it is not the event that caused those feelings, but your thoughts about the event. It is an indication that you must DO something to be able to overcome those thoughts.

When you receive unwelcome news, do not deny the event actually happened. Accept it. Process the thought and get in touch with your feelings and emotions. Just do not live there. Allow it to pass. You should not think it is the end of your story. It is our thinking about an event that can lead us away from our destiny.

What can you do? Practice adding a new set of positive thoughts to your arsenal of wrong thinking:

*"No matter what I do,
I can't get ahead or do enough."*

*"...so, I will learn to do the right thing
and that will put me ahead of most and that
will be more than enough."*

*"If I have all that I really want, people
will be jealous of me."*

*"Jealousy is just another form of flattery.
They too agree that I am blessed to have
my desires and needs met."*

"No one loves me for myself."

*"I am loved by me and God. As soon as others
realize that they will love me, too."*

"Everybody can't be rich,
there isn't enough money for everyone."

"But there is certainly more than enough for me!"

"It is what it is!"

"But nothing is permanent.
Things can change in a moment."

Before you try to change your thoughts, begin by adding to them positive affirmations to change their meaning and intent. Do this every time a bad feeling comes over you. You will soon change dwelling on the negative into an opportunity to live positively and on purpose. ***Do it!***

You Can Change Your Thinking

It is said, "If you keep doing what you are doing, you will keep getting what you are getting." Since everything we do begins with a thought, we must be careful to think correctly and accurately. If we keep thinking what we are thinking, we will keep doing what we are doing and therefore we will keep getting what we are getting. Unless you are satisfied with living as you are and have accomplished living on purpose, change your thoughts.

We must change what we are thinking. Some of us have thought incorrectly for so long that these thoughts seem right. We have developed a way of thinking that has shaped our lives, as we know it. We have become accustomed to how and what we think and have settled comfortably with the failed results.

That is why some say, "Nothing good ever happens to me," or "People will always disappoint you, so don't depend on anyone." "I don't believe God can use me in a great way; that's for others." "I don't know why God let that happen to me." These thoughts play like a broken record in the minds of many.

As a result of this kind of toxic thinking, we live life always expecting dreadful things to happen and people to disappoint. We do not expect greatness in our lives and so we settle for mediocrity. We blame God for the missed opportunities, the frustrations, and the failures we experience, and what seems to be unanswered prayer. We think there is something wrong around us when it is actually something wrong within us. We need to change our way of thinking.

> *"If you keep doing what you are doing, you will keep getting what you are getting."*

Expect Good Gifts from the Father

We are all created in the image of God. We are made to be creative beings, co-creators with the Master Creator. We have access to all good things by merely asking. Do you believe that?

Matthew 7: 7-8 says: *"Keep on asking, and you will receive what you ask for. Keep on seeking, and you will find. Keep on knocking, and the door will be opened to you. For everyone who asks, receives. Everyone who seeks, finds. And to everyone who knocks, the door will be opened."*

Do just that. Since we receive in life what we expect out of life, raise your expectations. Keep asking until you receive what you thought you would never have; keep seeking and you will discover opportunities where you never imagined; keep knocking until what you believed to be a locked door swings open with possibilities beyond measure. The key word is keep, which means "to cause to continue in a given position, state, course, or action." You must not stop until the results are evident. You must expect these things to happen for you and they will. Continue asking, seeking, and knocking. ***Do it!***

Matthew 7: 9-11 continues, *"You parents–if your children ask for a loaf of bread, do you give them a stone instead? Or if they ask for a fish, do you give them a snake? Of course not! So, if you sinful people know how to give good gifts to your children, how much more will your heavenly Father give good gifts to those who ask him."*

> *"Change is difficult.*
> ***It takes work."***

Our dominant thoughts will always be reflected in our lives. If we think thoughts that lead us away from God's intention for our lives, we will be lead away. If we continue to think we are not what we are created to be, we will become just that – what we are not created to be. Let us intentionally think thoughts that are true and that lead us to our purpose.

The terrible things that happen to us all do not reflect our nature or relationship with our Creator. They are our circumstances. Our thoughts enable us to overcome the worst of circumstances if we think accurately.

It is not what happens to us that challenge us to stay in proper relationship with God, but our reaction to what happens. We think our way out of position. We lose our belief in the goodness of God. We lose our faith because of our thoughts. We give up and stop expecting good things.

Paul says in Philippians 4: 12-13, *"I know how to live on almost nothing or with everything. I have learned the secret of living in every situation, whether it is with a full stomach or empty, with plenty or little. For I can do everything through Christ, who gives me strength."*

We too must learn how to hold on to our position as creative purposeful people. We do not have to become devastated when devastating things happen to us. We can adjust our physical reality without losing our mental and spiritual resolve. We can do all that is presented to us to do as we rely on, trust in and cling to the Spirit of Christ within us that works on our behalf.

We must recognize that our thinking either moves us toward accomplishing our purpose or leads us further away. It can prevent us from becoming what we were created to be or cause us to embrace our true nature as spiritual beings in a physical body. It can cause us to either fear our future and relive our past or live in the present in spite of our present circumstances. Our thinking enslaves us or sets us free. If what you are thinking is not helping you, you must change the way you think.

It Takes Work to Change Your Mind

Change is difficult. It takes work. We must be willing to change our thinking and committed to doing the work to accomplish this important, life-giving task.

We have never actually thought about what it means to change our thinking. In the New Testament, both John the Baptist and Jesus proclaim the same message: "Repent, for the Kingdom of *God is at hand."* The word repent has been defined to mean, "feel sorry for what you have done." This leads us to believe repentance involves changing one's behavior. However, the actual meaning has less to do with changed behavior and more with changed thinking. The word repentance means "to constantly change one's mind." The word translated repent in the English New Testaments is the Greek word "metanoia."

W. E. Vine's New Testament Greek Grammar and Dictionary defines "metanoia" to mean "to perceive afterwards," hence it signifies to change one's mind or purpose, and it always involves a change for the better. Changing one's mind usually changes one's behavior.[1]

Many sincere people have lived years in frustration with the contradiction of feeling sorrow for their behavior yet continuing to act the same way as before "repenting." Attempt after failed attempt leaves us thinking, "Well, no one is perfect," but still wanting to change and believing in repentance. Change begins in our mind, with our thoughts.

This is why it is crucial to our wellbeing and our living on purpose to know what is true as opposed to what we think is true. We follow the followers, passing down the errors of those who erred before us. We have many tools today to enable us to know properly and accurately what the Word says and means.

The Amplified version of 2 Timothy 2:15 reads, *"Study and be eager and do your utmost to present yourself to God approved (tested by trial), a workman who has no cause to be ashamed, correctly analyzing and accurately dividing [rightly handling and skillfully teaching] the Word of Truth."*

> *"Doing is the application of knowledge, which is wisdom."*

We must be eager to do all we can to be all we can, as God has purposed us. There has to be a passion to know the truth. We must want truth more than tradition. In order to obtain truth, we must dare to be different and be willing to let go of wrong thinking, which produces wrong actions.

The Amplified Version of John 8:31B-32 tells us how to know Truth. *"If you abide in My word [hold fast to My teachings and live in accordance with them], you are truly My disciples. And you will know the Truth, and the Truth will set you free."*

"Abide in My word," does not mean to occasionally read the Word; it does not mean to aimlessly open, point and shoot at the scripture, nor does it mean to exclusively wait upon our leaders to feed to us their interpretation, (right or wrong), of what God has for His people.

"Abide[2] in My word," does mean to remain, continue, stay; to put up with, tolerate, stand, endure, sustain, or withstand without yielding or submitting; to wait for, await, to accept without opposition or question; to pay the price or penalty of; suffer for.

Look up "abide" in any collegiate dictionary. We live by what we think it means. Many have missed the truth of that verse and that is why truth is not known.

Knowing the truth hangs on two words that many have overlooked: "if" and "and." Knowing truth is conditional on "if" you abide (see definition above). If you have the ability to remain, wait for however long it takes, continue until it hurts, do whatever it takes, pay the price or penalty for, and willingness to suffer, if need be, AND (not optional) DO — "live in accordance with them."

If we are not living in accordance with the teachings that exist for us to follow, then we cannot expect to know truth. Doing is a by product of knowing. Doing is the application of knowledge, which is wisdom. One who is not wise, that is, knows what to do and does not do it, is by definition foolish.

Matthew 7:24-27 states: *"Anyone who listens to my teaching and follows it is wise, like a person who builds a house on solid rock. Though the rain comes in torrents and the floodwaters rise and the winds beat against that house, it will not collapse because it is built on bedrock.*

But anyone who hears my teaching and does not obey it is foolish, like a person who builds a house on sand. When the rains and floods come and the winds beat against that house, it will collapse with a mighty crash."

No matter how many motivational books or scripture you read, study, and memorize, if YOU are not DOING the work, you will not fully benefit. You must DO what you know. If you know and do not do, you are foolishly turning away the freedom to live and be as God has created you. You are simply exchanging the truth for a lie. Truth will cause you to be set free from the constraints holding you back from your destiny.

"If you abide in My word [hold fast to My teachings and live in accordance with them], you are truly My disciples. And you will know the Truth, and the Truth will set you free."

> *"To change our **thinking**, we must change our **perspective**."*

We cannot clearly see what God has for us or what our purpose truly is until we adjust our thinking. Our thinking is out of focus. Our imagination has become blurred because of our circumstances and changing situations.

We think old thoughts, repeating what we thought in the past instead of repenting to think anew. We hold on to traditions and old ways of thinking and allow our very purpose for living to slip out of our grip. We figuratively "cut the end of the ham off, throw it away and put it in a roasting pan" that is now large enough to accommodate any size ham without trimming.

To change our thinking, we must change our perspective. Most of us have a good idea of the way the world thinks because we study it daily by watching TV, consuming cable, and online programming, listening to world views by radio, reading newspapers and books, and engaging in discussions with others whose minds are shaped by the same.

We are consumed with entertainment, sports and talk shows. We spend hours on end with DVDs, TiVo, Wii in HD so we can LOL! When do we take time to quietly sit and meditate on what is true, and honorable, and right, and pure, and lovely, and admirable?

> *"Once we **change** our way of thinking, we need to learn how to **maintain it.**"*

Romans 12:2 tells us, *"Do not copy the behavior and customs of this world, but let God transform you into a new person by changing the way you think. Then you will learn to know God's will for you, which is good, pleasing, and perfect."*

We undoubtedly are shaped and influenced by what we take into, process, and accept in our mind as truth. We almost never give it a second thought, as we desire to be "in the know" as others are. We view the most horrendous local and world events with dull acceptance as the way things are.

Allow your mind to be transformed to see things from a spiritual point of view instead of a physical or worldly view. We need to consistently feed our mind with spiritual food.

Focus Your Thoughts

Philippians 4:8 reads: *"And now, dear brothers and sisters, one final thing. Fix your thoughts on what is true, and honorable, and right, and pure, and lovely, and admirable."*

Once we change our way of thinking, we need to learn how to maintain it. Fix means to put into permanent form; to make rigid or definite. Do not second-guess an accurate thought. Do not change your mind once your mind has been changed for the better. In other words, stay focused on the correct thought.

Ever notice that when you hold an uninterrupted thought for a brief period of time, your mind begins to produce other related reinforcing thoughts? The longer you hold the same thought, whether positive or negative, the more thoughts that are similar are formed in your mind. Eventually it becomes difficult to "derail" that train of thinking.

It takes us on a mental ride, a movie short, a daydream of our own choosing that is either blissful or nightmarish, depending on the first thought.

By fixing our thoughts, it makes our belief (faith) in that thought stronger. Many of us believe, at first, even what seems impossible. But as time passes, and sometimes in extraordinarily little time, (actually seconds), our belief turns to unbelief, thereby negating or preventing the impossible from happening. An excellent example can be found in the following account in Mark 9:16-27 about Jesus' disciples attempting to heal a young boy.

"What is all this arguing about?" Jesus asked. One of the men in the crowd spoke up and said, "Teacher, I brought my son so you could heal him. He is possessed by an evil spirit that will not let him talk. ...So, I asked your disciples to cast out the evil spirit, but they could not do it."

Jesus said to them, "You faithless people! How long must I be with you? How long must I put up with you? Bring the boy to me." So, they brought the boy. But when the evil spirit saw Jesus, it threw the child into a violent convulsion, and he fell to the ground, writhing and foaming at the mouth... "Have mercy on us and help us if you can."

"What do you mean, 'If I can'?" Jesus asked. "Anything is possible if a person believes. "The father instantly cried out, "I do believe, but help me overcome my unbelief!"

Of course, the end of the story is that the young boy was completely healed. It was their unbelief that cancelled the miracle that was past due.

How many times have we smiled inside as we see ourselves doing what we were created to do? The image of a success-ful future flickers briefly only to be snatched away by some uninvited, negative thought. How rude!

We must learn how to nail down our positive thoughts and desires. We must "super glue" them to our emotions to be able to carry them through the doubtful times. Attach those thoughts to a pleasant or passionate feeling. Associate what you imagine doing with joy and love. Feel that wonderful, giggle-producing image in your belly so that it sticks, no matter what. Do what-ever you can to FIX THAT THOUGHT!

Fix your thoughts and imagine the end of the story. All the events in between will try to distract and disrupt your original thought. Practice keeping your thoughts fixed and along with it, your belief (faith) in the end of your story. DON'T SECOND GUESS! Go with your first mind.

> ## "*Practice* thinking *what is* **honorable.**"

Practice thinking

Like the little engine that could repeated, "I think I can, I think I can, I think I can," we, too, should practice what we think.

Again, Philippians 4:8 reminds us: *"And now, dear brothers and sisters, one final thing. Fix your thoughts on what is true, and honorable, and right, and pure, and lovely, and admirable. Think about things that are excellent and worthy of praise."*

Choose anyone, several, or all of the positive areas that Paul suggests we fix our thoughts on and practice thinking them.

Practicing thinking what is true. "The economy is horrible! We are in terrible shape. How are we going to survive?" Are those true statements? To one neighbor with a job, we are in a recession. To you who are unemployed, it is a depression. But to another who seeks and finds opportunities to prosper especially during tough economic times, it is a gold mine.

Find out what is true and practice thinking that. Think, "I'll prosper in the Kingdom where I live, when I discover my purpose, no matter what it looks like." "I wonder what God has for me to do? I cannot wait to discover it, especially during these times!" "I think I'll be a blessing to others no matter what my condition is." Are any of those thoughts true for you? If not, then produce thoughts that are true for you and practice thinking them!

> *"Practice thinking what is right."*

What is always true is Psalm 37:3-5: *"Trust (lean on, rely on, and be confident) in the Lord and do good; so, shall you dwell in the land and feed surely on His faithfulness, and truly you shall be fed."*

"Delight yourself also in the Lord, and He will give you the desires and secret petitions of your heart."

"Commit your way to the Lord [roll and repose each care of your load on Him]; trust (lean on, rely on, and be confident) also in Him and He will bring it to pass." (Amplified Bible)

Practice thinking what is honorable. This is honest, fair thinking; or having integrity in one's beliefs and actions. "No one is fair today; everyone is out for themselves and out to get all you have. Look at how crooked people are in business, the church, and politics." If you cannot think of anyone who is honorable, make up an honorable moment and think of that.

"Wouldn't it be great if..."

To think about what is honorable, we need to find honor and integrity within ourselves. Rather than thinking about failures and our lack of integrity, we should think about and list our successes.

Remember the time you returned the extra change to the cashier who made a mistake or found something that was not yours and located its rightful owner? Think about the time you could have done the wrong thing but chose to do what was right.

Practice thinking what is right. It is right to think well of others, in spite of their unethical behavior. It is right to believe the best in others instead of the worst. There are many ways to see a situation, and everyone is entitled to an opinion. A person who starts a conversation with, "If I were you, I would..," is taking away your right to your opinion or perspective. Until their way is proven to be the only way, they must be open to and allow suggestions from others.

To be right is defined as, "correct in judgment, opinion, or action." Recall the times you or others were absolutely correct in these areas. The time your husband, wife, partner, or friend was right in what they said or did, or their perception of a situation. Think about that and smile. Be grateful for having that person in your life. Practice thinking about those moments.

Practice thinking what is pure. Pure is defined as "free from anything of a different, inferior, or contaminating kind." We start having a pure thought and then a "but" gets in there and muddies the water.

Eliminate the "buts" in your thinking. "I would love to do that, BUT I..." "I'm certain I could accomplish this, BUT I..." "I think God is leading me to do, go, or say...BUT I!"

"Buts" contaminate pure thoughts. When a "BUT I" shows up in your thought, immediately look that BUT directly in the "I" and replace "I" with the word "nothing." "I would love to do that, BUT NOTHING..." "I'm certain I could accomplish this, BUT NOTHING..." "I think God is leading me to do, go, or say...BUT NOTHING!"

"There will be nothing added that will contradict or diminish the thought that will lead me to fulfilling my purpose." Practice thinking that.

Practice thinking what is admirable, that is "worthy of admiration, inspiring approval, reverence, or affection. Excellent; first-rate."

Is there anything or anyone that you admire? Look closely around you. Is there a relative, friend, coworker, fellow classmate, military personnel, spiritual leader, service worker, doctor, dentist, public speaker, technician, entertainer, public worker, author, teacher, songwriter, artist, poet, or anyone you know that is worthy of inspiring approval or reverence? Think for a moment. What makes them stand out in your mind? Why them? What have they done or are presently doing that you admire?

Thinking what is admirable about someone else should inspire you to be the kind of person that someone else can say, "That person is first-rate. They are excellent, no matter what they are doing." Thinking precedes doing. If you think about what is worthy of admiration, sooner or later you will be doing what is also admirable. Practice thinking admirable thoughts.

Practice makes perfect. That is not an absolutely true statement. If that were true, professional athletes would never botch a play or drop a ball; musicians would never hit a wrong note, and actors would never flub a line. Practice makes PERMANENT. The repetitive action is recorded in your mind until it is performed automatically, not perfectly.

> *"Practice thinking what is admirable."*

When you practice thinking accurate thoughts over and over again, you will soon always think thoughts that will lead you to fulfilling your purpose in life. That pattern of thinking will become permanent.

I have been thinking, "I am an author, I can write, I can produce a book" (ask those who know me), and here it is. Finished, published, and being read by many of you I have not yet met. By no means was it an easy project. I had to get through many mental and physical obstacles. I have learned how to practice thinking positive thoughts and embracing my purpose in life. It initially became real, not on paper, but in my mind. I had to practice the thought of being a published author until it became permanent in my spirit.

Those who are spiritually connected to The Creator of all things and the source of all positive thoughts, please listen to that "still, small voice," and hold on to the message. Fix it firmly in your mind and practice thinking it over and over until it is permanent. Then watch what happens!

Practice thinking what is true, and honorable, and right, and pure, and lovely, and admirable. ***Do it now!***

Throw out negative thoughts

We must learn how to throw out thoughts that do not serve our purpose. We blame a lot on others and outside forces, but we alone are responsible for the thoughts that we keep. For so long we have practiced discarding great ideas that come from God, while keeping the thoughts that cause us to worry and fret over future events that may never happen and that usually do not.

> *"Get rid of*
> *negative thoughts."*

Think to yourself, "No, I do not like the way that thought makes me feel. I do not agree with that. Out you go!" Then replace it with a beautiful, wonderful thought that will cause you to feel ecstatic. Write that thought on a card and keep it with you. It is a place you want to or have visited. It is an experience you would love to have like riding a motorcycle or growing a flower or vegetable garden. It is cooking that perfect pot of beans! Pull out that card and read it every time you have one of those bothersome thoughts.

Whenever I get a flashing thought of impending financial ruin, I immediately think to myself, "I've got much more money than I'll ever need, and I feel GOOD about it!" Then I confirm that with Philippians 4:19, which says: "And this same God who takes care of me will supply all your needs from his glorious riches, which have been given to us in Christ Jesus."

You positively must get rid of negative thoughts as soon as they enter your mind. Many visions are brought to naught, not for lack of vision but simply because of "stinkin' thinkin'". Take the garbage out! It will contaminate your entire being when it contaminates your thoughts. The longer you wait, the more damaging that thought will become.

Have an arsenal of affirmations ready to fire on any negative thought that rears its ugly head. Kill it at all costs.

Think God thoughts

Change your mind from the way you think to the way God thinks. Some who just read this will think, "I can't think like God." To whom do you attribute the thoughts you have? Either they came from you or from somewhere else. That somewhere else is either in this world or somewhere higher.

Isaiah 55:8-9 reads: *"My thoughts are completely different from yours," says the LORD. "And my ways are far beyond anything you could imagine. For just as the heavens are higher than the earth, so are my ways higher than your ways and my thoughts higher than your thoughts."*

That is an agreeable statement to many who dare not believe they can actually think the thoughts of God. It seems out of reach to try to think like God thinks when it is said how different his thoughts are from ours.

We go through life wanting more, wanting answers, daring to dream big, but not too big, but still are frustrated and empty because we cannot reach our fullest potential. We continue to dismiss anything that seems lofty and settle for a mundane mediocre existence. Our purpose for living is right there in front of us, but we continue to think more "normal" and less spiritual.

"For those who are according to the flesh and are controlled by its unholy desires set their minds on and pursue those things which gratify the flesh, but those who are according to the Spirit and are controlled by the desires of the Spirit set their minds on and seek those things which gratify the [Holy] Spirit." – Romans 8:5 (Amplified Bible)

It is easy to tell our thoughts apart from God's thoughts. Ours usually spin us into a frenzy over future things we think may happen to us based on our present circumstance or past experiences. Other people influence our thinking to be competitive, (keeping up with the Jones') or selfish, (grab all the gusto you can get.) Many of us subscribe to the "have it your way" school of thought. However, 1 Corinthians 2:9-12, 16 tells us:

"No eye has seen,
no ear has heard,
and no mind has imagined
what God has prepared for
those who love him."

"But it was to us that God revealed these things by his Spirit. For his Spirit searches out everything and shows us God's deep secrets. No one can know a person's thoughts except that person's own spirit, and no one can know God's thoughts except God's own Spirit. And we have received God's Spirit (not the world's spirit), so we can know the wonderful things God has freely given us.

For, "Who can know the Lord's thoughts? Who knows enough to teach him?" But we understand these things, for we have the mind of Christ."

If something is beneficial to someone else before you and takes dedication and determination to see the vision through, it came from some outside intelligence, namely The Mind of Christ.

> *"Many of us only think*
> ***selfish thoughts."***

We, who accept this belief, have The Mind of Christ. There is a popular bracelet imprinted with the saying, "What would Jesus do" (WWJD). How about, "What would Jesus think?"

1 Corinthians 2:16 reads: *"Who can know the Lord's thoughts? Who knows enough to teach him? But we understand these things, for we have the mind of Christ."*

Who can have a Christ Mind? Those who accept the Spirit that comes from God into their being and allow the thoughts which the Spirit brings into their mind. Thinking, knowing, and acting upon these thoughts transforms the mind to see things from a spiritual perspective.

> *"Rejoice in*
> *the thoughts*
> *of possibilities."*

A Christ Mind produces thoughts that are unselfish and loving without condition – thoughts of concern for others before oneself. If you think that way, you can be used in an unlimited and unusual capacity. That kind of mind will produce those things that benefit your family, your community, and your world.

Many of us only think selfish thoughts: "How will this benefit ME?" "I'm waiting for my ship to come in, so I can enjoy my life." "I must do for me and then I can do for others."

The mind of Christ thinks loving thoughts that are unselfish, unconditional, and unlimited. *"I can do ALL THINGS through Christ who gives me the strength."* –Philippians 4:13

We limit our thoughts, thereby limiting the positive impact we can have on society. If our thoughts were on a menu, many of us would choose what we could afford instead of what we desire to eat. Look at the menu and choose what fits your taste. You do not have to be wasteful or extravagant, but order what you want! If you want lobster, order it! If you have a taste for roast duck, then you should request it. If there were no prices on the menu, wouldn't you pick what best fulfilled you? We limit our thoughts by what we see or the resources we have. We cannot imagine what was meant when Jesus said in John 14:12: *"and greater works than these shall he do."* He was speaking of others doing what he did and even greater. He said it was because he was going to the Father on our behalf.

Go ahead and order the meal of your choosing. You do not have to be concerned with catching, cleaning, or preparing the meat. You do not have to grow the vegetables or be skilled in culinary arts. Just joyfully order the meal. The waiter will relay your request to the cook, who is more than prepared to give you your stomach's (heart's) desire.

Again, Psalms 37:4 tells us to *"Delight yourself also in the Lord, and He will give you the desires and secret petitions of your heart."* There is infinite supply to do all that you desire to do when you think thoughts with the Mind of Christ.

We think of all the reasons why we cannot "DO," instead of rejoicing in the thoughts of possibility, not our possibility, but God's possibility. This is predicated upon us cooperating by repenting or changing our way of thinking from the human mind to a spiritual mind.

Control Your Emotions and Feelings

Exercise control over your emotions. Emotions are indicators of what is going on in your life. They give insight as to how we react on the inside to what is happening on the outside. They are not who you are, but simply how you are at a given moment. You are sad, angry, excited, or motivated because of your environment. Your life is talking to you.

Learn to express your emotions appropriately and how to hold on to those that will serve your purpose best. Stay motivated and excited as long as possible, especially through the challenging times. Take time to think and note what causes your emotions to become active. What actually turns them on? The conditions for fear, joy, love, sadness, surprise, or anger may be different for you than someone else. Make a note the next time your emotions surface. Write it down. "I get angry every time..." "I sense fear whenever..." "This really brings me joy."

Review your findings and make changes in your life where necessary. If television news makes you sad, do not watch it. If sending cards to encourage others brings you joy, find inexpensive ways to continue doing that more often.

If you find yourself constantly getting angry for little or no reason, or you feel the need to retaliate every chance you get, you may want to look more closely into the cause. It may be thoughts stemming from past experiences of being taken advantage of or thoughts of revenge. Harboring unforgiveness can also play a role in being angry.

This book, however, is not a counseling treatise, but rather one intended to heighten your awareness of yourself in regard to fulfilling your purpose. There may be times when spending time with people more skilled in this area is warranted. If necessary, seek help. ***Do it!***

As spiritual people, we have access to many tools that enable us to get a handle on our emotions. Words found in the scriptures can be an immediate source of enlightenment and resolution to our emotional dilemma. Find words that will encourage you to accept and tend to your emotions, such as "Perfect love expels all fear" (I John 4:18). Where love is perfected or matured in your life, fear is no longer present.

Philippians 4:6-7 reads: *"Do not be anxious about anything, but in every situation, by prayer and petition, with thanksgiving, present your requests to God. And the peace of God, which transcends all understanding, will guard your hearts and your minds in Christ Jesus."*

"Don't be dejected and sad, for the joy of the Lord is your strength!" – Nehemiah 8:10

1 Peter 4:12-13 & 19 reads: *"Dear friends, do not be surprised at the fiery trials you are going through, as if something strange were happening to you. Instead, be very glad – for these trials make you partners with Christ in his suffering. So, if you are suffering in a manner that pleases God, keep on doing what is right, and trust your lives to the God who created you, for he will never fail you."*

"And "do not sin by letting anger control you. Do not let the sun go down while you are still angry, for anger gives a foothold to the devil." – Ephesians 4:26-27

Do not try to ignore your emotions and feelings. You do not have to act on them, but you do have to recognize their existence. It is potentially dangerous to suppress your feelings. Find a way to wisely express your emotions and feelings. Keep in mind you do not want to sabotage your purpose. Untamed emotions can easily bring your destiny to a crashing halt.

Practice saying what you are feeling and what emotion may be associated with it. When you get disturbing financial news, you may feel sick to your stomach. The emotion could be surprised or fear and anger. Once you can identify what you are feeling and what emotions are triggered, you can then decisively apply the proper treatment.

Use your emotions as indicators that something is happening inside of you. We often ignore the signs until things are out of control. We continue ignoring our melancholy mood until it turns into deep sadness, which if left unattended, turns into depression.

Remember, your thoughts control your feelings and emotions. They contribute to what you may feel about where you are in life, both in a positive and negative way. If you think positively, as often as possible, you will feel optimistic even when people, events and circumstances are unfavorable.

> *"Color makes a significant impact on our mood."*

Feel your way to fulfilling your purpose

Feelings can be used to push our purpose to fulfillment. Having passion, poise and perseverance will help weather the storms that are sure to come our way. We must unleash positive emotions and feelings to work on our behalf. We need to be motivated, get inspiration and have enthusiasm. All these are essential in bringing our purpose to completion.

Let's get motivated! Motivation is the driving force that causes us to push toward fulfilling our purpose. Motivation, although not an emotion, is related to one's emotions.

With proper motivation, we will begin to move from creative thought to determined action. Once we are highly motivated and our purpose is clear and focused, there is little that can prevent success.

We can be motivated both intrinsically or from within, and extrinsically, from outside sources. We must be aware of those around us who are not in favor or not clear of our mission. Do not try to convince them. Our purpose is better shown than shared; it is easier caught than taught. Once they see it in motion or after completion, they will have a better "feel" for what we have been excited about all along.

We must be aware of our surroundings. It is difficult to get motivated and stay that way for any length of time if the conditions around you are dismal. It is important to work in a clean, neat environment, free of clutter and chaos. If possible, have live plants or pets, such as a small aquarium with betta fish, in sight. If not, place artificial plants or pictures of nature in your workspace within your line of sight.

Color, although sometimes overlooked, is important in setting the mood for motivation. Color makes a significant impact on our mood and can evoke an emotion or feeling. Use of color can transform your space with depth, feeling, and power.

The color yellow sets a tone of warmth, motion, cheerfulness, and friendliness. It gives us the feeling that we get from the sunshine. However, like the sun, the color yellow should be used sparingly and not too intensely. As too much sun can cause burned skin, too much yellow in our surroundings can create anxiety.

> *"Your thoughts control your feelings and emotions."*

Orange is known to strengthen our concentration and to promote a sense of purpose. It helps to get our creative juices flowing when they become stagnant.

Blue is calming and soothing. It creates a feeling of peace and trust. Ocean and sky-blue scenes are often seen in work areas. These shades of blue are representative of adventure and exploration, while navy blue is the color of intellect and wisdom.

White color represents poise, confidence, and purity. In combination with gold or silver, it tends to generate a calm, serene atmosphere.1

Not only do we have to pay attention to our physical surroundings, but we must also be aware of our inner sanctum—that private place where your dreams are born, and your destiny lies. If it is full of clutter or over saturated with disturbing, muted thoughts, chances are you will not be very motivated.

You must make your internal workspace conducive to motivation. Take time to simplify your thought life. While waiting on your purpose to be fulfilled, limit your intake of mental simulation that does not support your purpose. Reduce the amount of time you spend on entertainment, video games, sporting events, shopping, mindless conversations, and other time wasters, which I call "mind wasters."

Carefully select what you take into your "inner" environment by way of music, books, television programming or the Internet. Limit conversing with negative people on a consistent basis. They can distract you from and rob you of essential motivation.

Keep the positive people who support your vision around you as much as possible. Do whatever it takes to protect your peace and receptiveness to positive, spiritual messages. It takes work. Do it and it will keep you poised for inspiration.

Get inspired! Let God breathe on it. Inspiration means "a breathing in" (as in respiration). The Greek word, Theo-pneustos means "God-breathed." Theo (God) and pneuma (wind, breathe) come from the root pneu, meaning dynamic movement of air. This 'air' does not speak of a gentle breeze; rather, it is the kind that blows with the intention of moving things around or causing something to happen.

It is used to describe the movement of air used to create music from a wind instrument. It can also be described as air or movement to project emotions such as fear, joy, love, sadness, surprise, or anger.

In order to activate your divine purpose, it is necessary to get motivated or "forced to drive." However, fear and greed can be that force. The fear of loss or the assurance of gain has motivated many individuals to excel in any given area.

To fulfill your divine purpose, you need positive motivation as well as inspiration, or the Spirit of God to blow on or in it to infuse it with life, force, life force, energy, and power. When this happens, music is in the air. Your positive emotions are activated, and your creative abilities become in harmony with your purpose. All around you seems to be in concert with what needs to be accomplished.

Do you ever notice how people who are extremely motivated, but not inspired, often become a pain to be around? They are forever driving forward their point, running people over with their mission and leaving "hit and run" victims strewn all over the road. You love and hate their appearances; hate to see them come and love to see them go.

When that same person is also inspired, the atmosphere is completely different. Inspiration creates an emotion of joy and love in the air. You can "feel" their mission and you want to play even a small part in this symphony of divinely inspired purpose.

It does not matter what the activity is. It can be collecting used clothing to give away or clipping coupons to buy essentials at a discount for the less fortunate. It does not have to be at a grand scale; it just has to be an inspired act. It all feels so moving that you want in. Be in a place where the wind of God blows best and watch how different your life and purpose will become! Get ready to get enthused.

Get enthusiastic, light a fire under it! "Catch fire with enthusiasm and people will come from miles to watch you burn." –John Wesley, founder of Methodism

The word enthusiasm comes from the ancient Greek word eufousiasmz. En Theos meaning "inspired by or possessed by God; full of God" or "the God within." It implies "an absorbing or controlling passion of the mind by any interest or pursuit." It can also imply being obsessed with a thought or idea one wishes to see to completion.

> ## *"The present gives us 'right now' feelings."*

Enthusiasm brings with it a oneness with God and the Spirit within us. As inspiration connotes harmony with purpose and spiritual life force, enthusiasm brings harmony between a person with purpose and the Creator. It brings both together into a wonderful relationship that affects everything we do.

People who have enthusiasm seem to be successful at all they do. You want to be around them to feel the passion, energy and excitement coming from within them. It is because they are intimately involved with their passion.

Enthusiasm is that passionate energy operating in its highest form. Enthusiasm is motivation and inspiration on steroids! It is beyond thrilling. Excitement is not an adequate word to describe the feeling you get when you are enthused. You actually become possessed by the feeling from within. It is not dependent on outside stimulus or circumstances; in fact, nothing can stop you once you get enthusiastic about your purpose.

To get enthused, you must have a desire for purpose in mind. Your thinking must be focused or fixed ON PURPOSE. Then, you must get motivated to act on that thought. Should inspiration come, it will bring clarity and inner peace to the process for reaching your goal. Enthusiasm assures you will not give up, no matter what. It will attract all you need and elicit spiritual support in harmony with your commitment to the feeling and doing in the present moment.

What we need to fully understand is that we are possessed with the awareness and feelings associated with what is happening in the present moment. Our past and future thoughts leave us with memories and dreams. However, the present gives us "right now" feelings from within that drive us relentlessly toward our goal. It is the feelings and emotions that are so powerful.

The present or as some call it, the "now moment" is the product of our belief or faith in the God breath or inspiration surrounding our purpose. Faith is the "now" substance of things hoped for in the future. Faith is the "now" evidence of things not seen yet but will manifest in the future. Enthusiasm lives in the now.

Intentionally feel passionate about your purpose. Have strong feelings about the present and attach joy and love to it. Love what you are created to be and do. Love the people you will affect when your divine purpose is in full operation. Be determined and devoted to excellence. Be diligent and disciplined in all you do.

Be certain you are sincere when displaying enthusiasm. If you are truly enthusiastic, it will be felt. You cannot fake its existence; sooner or later your movement towards your goal will cease if you are insincere.

In the meantime, while you are waiting for faith to produce your dream and divine destiny, be content with where you are and what you have. Do not be envious of nor compare your vision to that of others around you. Your life's goal is not a competition. It is a long-distance run with only you in the race.

> *"Intentionally feel passionate about your purpose."*

Choose your words wisely

Watch your words! Words are immensely powerful, so choose them wisely. Before we utter the thought, consider the effect it will have on your purpose. We sometimes shoot ourselves in the foot by speaking against our own interests. Speak words that are positive and affirming that will push forward your purpose in life. Speak these words with emotion and speak them often. Watch your words and watch what happens!

Be sure you are speaking out of a pure heart, one that is infused with inspiration and displays enthusiasm. When talking about your divine purpose, be careful with your words. When your words are sprinkled with uncertainty and negativity concerning your goals, it reveals that your heart is not prepared for your purpose.

Words come from the heart

Matthew 12:33 reads: *"A tree is identified by its fruit. If a tree is good, its fruit will be good. If a tree is bad, its fruit will be bad. For whatever is in your heart determines what you say."*

No matter what your intentions are – good, bad, or indifferent – words that are significant and carried by emotions come from your heart.

Some have made a horrible practice of saying negative, harsh words as commentary to what others say and do. They are critical and condescending. Seldom are they kind and encouraging. They automatically deliver a striking blow with an unkind word, negative comment, or scathing remark to everyone that crosses their path.

"I wouldn't do that if I were you." "Why didn't you tell me about that before?" "That won't work; you are wasting your time." They are no longer aware of the impact their words have because of years of practicing that negative habit. There may be an issue with them feeling the pinch of their own unfulfilled lives and want you to continue life status quo. It is easier to attack than to admit.

Do not be one of them. Do not allow them to influence your thinking or actions. If you are to fulfill your purpose, you must be aware of every word you speak, and the words spoken around you.

Speak your way to fulfilling your purpose

Speak to yourself first, then to others. Learn and use words to encourage yourself. Do not talk yourself out of your divine purpose. Most times, we are our own worst enemy. We stop a few words short of our goal because we have not learned the value of speaking into our own lives.

"Self-talk" is an effective tool to speak positively toward fulfilling our purpose. No one else but you are with you "twenty-four-seven." During those twenty-four hours, spend time speaking out loud words that are positive, encouraging, and spiritual to yourself. We curse and complain out loud when the opportunity arises. We are quick to blurt out negative responses to an event. Why not reverse the trend? Blurt out a positive comment like, "Wow, this book I'm writing is fantastic!" or "I AM a good writer after all!"

> *"Speak affirmations that will lead you to fulfilling your purpose."*

In fact, hardly anyone would notice if you blurted something out in public because of everyone on their cell phones with discreet listening devices placed in their ear. Join the crowd!

But seriously, take some time ALONE and speak out loud to yourself. Do not wait until you are discouraged and lack enthusiasm. Speak now while you are on point so that you can stay on point.

Speak affirmations that will lead you to fulfilling your purpose. This is not the time for complaints or selfish requests. Use scripture, words of wisdom and encouragement from those you admire or create your own personal affirmations.

Start with gratitude. "I am sooooo thankful for another day topside!" "This is the day that the Lord has made; I will rejoice and be glad in it." "I am grateful to spend another great day in the Kingdom!"

> ## *"Watch what you say AND to whom you say it.."*

Continue with recognition of who you are. "I am a new creation in Christ; the old is gone, the new has come." "I am eternal, immortal, universal, and infinite; my expectations are truly limitless."

Then speak in recognition of who God is. "Father, I am grateful for how you have made me intentionally and with personal care. You are all powerful, all knowing, and infinitely wise. I know that You are the Supreme Source and Giver of every good and perfect gift. Thank you for the gift of _____ you have given to me."

Speak Words of encouragement. "I can do all things through the Christ spirit within me, with the Christ mind that strengthens my resolve to live my purpose. There is nothing nor no one who will stand in my way of fulfilling what is divinely mine to complete."

Release and expect. Let go and let God do what you are confident He can and will accomplish. Do not be surprised. Expect to see and feel the unusual and unpredictable begin to happen.

Watch what you say AND to whom you say it.

When we are in process of discovering and fulfilling our purpose, we sometimes believe others will be as excited and enthused as we are. However, sadly enough, that is not the case. There will be those who are close to you that will not celebrate to see the change in you. They will not only NOT support you but may actually attempt to undermine your efforts.

This is a crucial point to remember. Not following this advice has caused many to give up or crippled them from continuing on because of the extreme, unexpected opposition that followed their innocent unveiling of purpose.

One of the best examples of this is found in Genesis 37. There begins the story of a young man, Joseph, who had a dream of what his purpose in life would be. He was not careful with whom he shared his important dream nor how he shared it, which resulted in the following:

Verse 3-11 reads, *"Jacob loved Joseph more than any of his other children because Joseph had been born to him in his old age. So, one day Jacob had a special gift made for Joseph— a beautiful robe. But his brothers hated Joseph because their father loved him more than the rest of them. They could not say a kind word to him.*

One night Joseph had a dream, and when he told his brothers about it, they hated him more than ever. "Listen to this dream," he said. "We were out in the field, tying up bundles of grain. Suddenly my bundle stood up, and your bundles all gathered around and bowed low before mine!"

His brothers responded, "So you think you will be our king, do you? Do you actually think you will reign over us?" And they hated him all the more because of his dreams and the way he talked about them.

Soon Joseph had another dream, and again he told his brothers about it. "Listen, I have had another dream," he said. "The sun, moon, and eleven stars bowed low before me!"

This time he told the dream to his father as well as to his brothers, but his father scolded him. "What kind of dream is that?" he asked. "Will your mother and I and your brothers actually come and bow to the ground before you?" But while his brothers were jealous of Joseph, his father wondered what the dreams meant."

The story continues in verses 18-24: *"When Joseph's brothers saw him coming, they recognized him in the distance. As he approached, they made plans to kill him. "Here comes the dreamer!" they said. "Come on, let us kill him and throw him into one of these cisterns. We can tell our father, 'A wild animal has eaten him.' Then we will see what becomes of his dreams!"*

So, when Joseph arrived, his brothers ripped off the beautiful robe he was wearing. Then they grabbed him and threw him into the cistern. Now the cistern was empty; there was no water in it."

Finally, verse 28 reads: *"So when the Ishmaelites, who were Midianite traders, came by, Joseph's brothers pulled him out of the cistern and sold him to them for twenty pieces of silver. And the traders took him to Egypt."*

Those who are closest to you, who know you better than most, are often the ones who have trouble accepting your dream and vision to be what God intended you to be.

The end of the story gives us hope that even in the face of extreme opposition, our purpose can be fulfilled. Joseph indeed did become a high-ranking official in Egypt and his family did live under his authority. When you accept your purpose in life, you will not have to wonder how it will be accomplished. Ready or not, with resources available or not, it will come to pass.

> # *"Get rid of negative thoughts."*

Use what you have

"But I am not skilled or highly equipped. I do not have the talents that others seem to have," you may think. What skill or service can you perform even as a novice? What is in your hand? Use what you have.

God posed that question to Moses after he discovered his purpose, which was to free the people from Egyptian bondage (Exodus 4). Moses had a stick; a large, ordinary stick. He used it as a staff to walk over rough terrain, to protect himself from wild animals and robbers, and to help save helpless animals from danger who had become trapped in otherwise unreachable places.

God did not say get a bigger stick, a better stick. He did not say, "That is all you have? A stick? You will need more than that!

You are to free over 600,000 people who want to worship Me freely in the desert instead of working as slaves in the mud pits of Egypt. Find a better instrument to use." No, God told Moses to "use what you have."

If we really think about it, we have enough time, money, education, help, knowledge, talent, and all the resources we need to complete our purpose in life. Whatever more we need, will be provided. We err because we usually do not start the process because we think we need more before we can begin. We change our mind and actions to fit what we THINK we need instead of expanding our thoughts to accommodate the Mind of Christ, which says: *"Ask and it will be given, seek and you will find, knock and the door will open."* –Matthew 7:7

> *"Find a place of comfort and free of distractions."*

What is in your hand? What skills and talents do you have? What desires do you have on hand for products to create or services to perform? What creative words or breathtaking images are at your fingertips ready to be put on paper or canvas, on stage or in song?

Discovering your purpose in life

You already know what your purpose in life is. You have known it since your birth. That knowledge has been with you daily and exists in everything you do. It is not to be confused with what you THINK your purpose is, nor what others think you should be doing with your life.

Your purpose is not what you would like to do to "make a living." It is not what you would like to do as a career, what your friends want you to help them with or to join them in doing.

Purpose is not what you go to school to become. It is not what catches your attention as something good to do with your life since you have nothing better to do. Purpose is not what your parents did and so you too should do the same.

Purpose IS what God has placed in your heart and your mind. It is your emotions and your thoughts from deep within. It will not go away or change. It is a permanent part of you. It is as unique as your fingerprint, your iris, your personality, your voice pattern and even your DNA. Your purpose is you.

Sometime shortly after birth, we become disconnected from that inner knowledge of our purpose. Our experiences have shaped us to become what we are not purposed to be. Our education has led us from our divine purpose to other interests. Our ego has influenced us to "be all that you can be" instead of "be all that you are purposed to be."

You have never considered how unique you really are. Before you, there has never been a you and after you, there will never be another. They truly did "break the mold" after you were created. If you do not discover, accept, and live out your purpose, no one else will.

As trivial as you may think what God has purposed you to do is, it is equally as significant as all others. Each grain of salt, although different, adds flavor and helps preserve where it is used. You cannot say that one grain of salt is more important or "saltier" than another.

We have had little or no assistance with moving us toward living outside the box where God joins us with inspiration and enthusiasm. We have been left to decide on our own the path we should take in life.

Some who already know their purpose are waiting for some best time to start. After their first career or after reaching a certain level of financial security. Others are waiting for some grand opportunity to come knocking on their door, including winning the lottery.

So, how do we discover our purpose? There are no perfect answers, and I am not an expert on the subject, by any means. By now, you should be adequately equipped to cut a clear path on which you can travel with deliberateness toward fulfilling your purpose. It would be best for you to find your own means of motivation to discover what is inside of you. But in case you have no idea where to start, begin with this straightforward process.

Find a place of comfort and free of distractions. One you can conveniently return to as often as necessary. Make sure your surroundings are suited for optimum motivation. Have a pad or notebook and pen or pencil with you. A laptop or other word processor can be useful but is not necessary.

Take all the time you need. Be serious. Do not rush through the process. Your concern is the discovery of your purpose, not completing a survey. If it takes days or weeks to complete the entire process that is fine. This could potentially make the difference for the rest of your life.

Think of and list at least ten purposes or careers in life that you know are NOT what you were born to fulfill. Start by writing, "I know I was NOT born to..." This is to purge you of any wrong ideas you may have had about your purpose.

Next, describe the characteristics of what you would like to do or be. Not the name of the job like police officer, teacher, scientist, or receptionist, but a description of what it is that you feel you want to do. "I would like to do something from 9 AM - 3 PM, 11 PM - 7 AM, long hours, part-time, on call, flexible schedule, outside, inside, traveling, in the city, in the suburbs, in the country, working with hundreds of different people, collaborating with a few co-workers, working alone, or working at home. I would like to own my own business, work for a small, private company, large corporation, the military, customer service, administrative, management or creative services."

"I would like to collaborate with people who are children, elderly, infants, adults, teens, athletes, creative, criminals, highly intelligent, learning disabled, needy, affluent, chronically ill, or extremely fit. I would like them to be men, women, African American, Asian, Hispanic, White, multi-cultural or religious."

"I would like to sing, dance, play an instrument, crunch numbers, fill out forms, talk on the phone, give speeches, fix things, break things, build, paint, clean, dirty, ride, drive, sit, walk fast paced or slow paced, wear casual clothing, business attire, run equipment, use a computer, lift, read, write, teach, learn, serve, counsel, be creative, cook or taste. I would like to be in an environment that is noisy, quiet, safe, dangerous, dark, bright, fun, serious, simple, or complex." Write down things like these, plus whatever else comes to your mind.

Have fun with it! Do not name the industry that exists. Just list the characteristics of what you would like to do. Spend lots of time and write whatever comes to mind no matter how silly it may seem to you. Continue until you are exhausted and can no longer think of another thing to write. If necessary, stop the process and come back to it later or the next day.

In the meantime, keep thinking of the type of things you would like to do. "I would really like to be around water, in the sun, dig in the dirt, landscape, plant flowers, vegetables, shrubs or trees. I could enjoy caring for animals like dogs, cats, fish, birds, reptiles, bugs, lions and tigers and bears, oh my!"

Once you have completed the list of characteristics or type of job you would like to do, read over the list several times. Now identify, (list, underline, or circle) the characteristics that cause you to feel something or move you in some way. When you read the list, identify what makes you smile or laugh or sigh. Skip the ones you listed that cause you negative reactions or no reaction at all. Note the ones that you "feel" something positive about.

Now write another list based on the items you highlighted from the first list. Get more specific and as detailed as you can. You will begin seeing something interesting about yourself. Of all the things you can think of doing, only some things really cause a positive reaction. You are beginning to feel what you would like to do. You are no longer thinking about how much money you can make, but rather what feels right, purposeful and fulfilling.

Start taking the information and begin building a statement that includes the words on your new list. It could sound something like this: "I would like to work downtown, with a few co-workers, who are culturally mixed, dress casually, use computers, in a creative services environment that is fast-paced, and allows me to have a flexible schedule with some travel."

> *"Purpose is being who you are*
> *— for free! "*

Now, imagine what your day would look like or more importantly, what it would feel like. "It feels good to get up and go downtown to be among hundreds of people, doing what I like to do, whatever that might be. I can imagine a fast-paced, large, noisy room with people moving about. My day would go so fast that I would be disappointed that it was over. I would look forward to coming in the next day or staying to work overtime." Record or write down how you would feel if given the list of things you would like to do.

Keep imagining until you feel really excited or passionate about it. If a negative thought enters your mind, throw it out or change the circumstances to bring you back to that enthusiastic wonderful place. See yourself doing what makes you feel fulfilled.

Now shift a bit to include others. Can what you describe being or doing be a benefit to someone else? In what way can you be fulfilled while benefiting others? What is it that you are doing that makes another person smile, laugh, feel grateful or ecstatic, or simply better than they did before you did what you do? What does that look like? What does that feel like?

The feeling of fulfillment comes from dropping children back home from school with your van service, the applause from the crowd after singing one of your favorite Ella Fitzgerald jazz tunes, reading excerpts from your latest book to a wide-eyed audience, or visiting an elderly parishioner who lights up every time she sees you. Or it could be all the discounted items you were able to buy and share with those in need because of your passion for clipping and using coupons! Feel the fulfillment, and you will discover your passion and purpose.

Your purpose is discovering not what makes you plenty of money, but what gives you plenty of passion! Purpose is what you get lost in doing; what you would work hard at EVERY SINGLE DAY. Purpose is what you would do to see the discouraged, confused, lifeless look on a person's face change to hopefulness, gratefulness and aglow with life because you touched their lives by being "who I am created to be." Purpose is being who you are – for free!

When is the last time you felt anything besides misery when you got up to go to work, school, church, the mall, back home from vacation or back home, period, or visit friends and family or anywhere alone? When is the last time you felt any joy or love in what you do? If you can identify with any of this, you can be sure that you have either forgotten or have never known what your purpose in life is.

Just think, if you discover your purpose and live on purpose, there will be one less miserable person on the planet that doesn't know or care why they exist; one less materialistic, selfish, superficial being, working hard for the money; one less poor person dying with a full financial portfolio and an empty, unfulfilled life; one less person who has only passed through life, never stopping to "smell the coffee" or enjoy a cup of coffee (or tea) with a friend.

Aren't you tired of wondering when things will get better, when better is nowhere in sight? Aren't you tired of the struggle to feel good about anything, especially waking up to the struggle to feel good about anything? Aren't you tired of the constant pressure of "fakin' the funk?" You need to pursue your passion and purpose until you find it!

Trust your passion! It will bring you wealth beyond measure, often monetary but always abundant, priceless fulfillment. You will be who you were created to be, void of hindrances. No circumstance nor situation, person or problem can prevent you from fulfilling your dream when infused with enthusiasm and passion. That IS the abundant life. "The thief's purpose is to steal and kill and destroy. My purpose is to give them a rich and satisfying life." –John 10:10

Write Your Vision and Make It Plain

Once your purpose is plain and your vision is clear, write it down so others can read it and understand. You MUST write it down. You will see it happen when you believe it can happen. Believing is seeing. Write it down. You will be taken seriously by the invisible forces at work when you have taken the time to write your vision. Unexpected events, serendipitous situations,

"Ron Moore moments" (sudden, synchronistic occurrences), and people of influence will miraculously show up to cause your vision to spring into action. All that you need will show up when you make plans on paper for it to happen.

When you write down your purpose and goals, there will be no mistakes in your intent. What you see, say, hear and feel changes over time. Our memory is affected by our circumstances and time. Over time, you cannot remember if you did something as a child or your sibling did it. But what you write lasts forever. It is an exact record. Write it down in detail. Review it periodically. Make updates and additions when necessary.

> "Keep *imagining* until you feel really excited or *passionate.*"

If you understand the importance of what you are to do with your life, and the impact you will have on your world around you, you will agree with the necessity to keep good records of the steps toward its completion.

Write down what you are feeling about your discovery of your purpose. "I feel excited now that I know I can help people to improve their finances." "I can't wait to read to my first elderly client."

Write down the period in which you would like things to happen. "In three weeks, I would like to have all the paperwork done to get my approval for my business loan." "In two months,

I would like to be in a position collaborating with creative people designing ads for non-profit organizations." "By next June, I would like to graduate from the program that will launch my career as a social worker or fire fighter or dietary aide."

Be as specific as possible but leave room for change. Imagine all that you need to accomplish your goal and write it down. If you need transportation or a building, write it down. If you need personnel, material donations, supplies, clients, customers, or specific connections, WRITE IT DOWN! Money is not the objective; your NEEDS will be supplied. If money is needed, it will come. Do not be concerned with how it will happen. Just enjoy the "feeling" of knowing it will happen.

"If you see it in your mind, you're going to hold it in your hand." –Bob Procter, The Secret *"And my God will liberally supply (fill to the full) your every need according to His riches in glory in Christ Jesus."* –Paul of Tarsus, Philippians 4:19 (Amplified Bible)

"If you live in Me [abide vitally united to Me] and My words remain in you and continue to live in your hearts, ask whatever you will, and it shall be done for you." –Jesus of Nazareth, John 15:7 (Amplified Bible)

Write when you would like to start. "I would like to begin part-time, the first week in June. By January, I would like to do this full-time."

Write all the cast of characters you would like to collaborate with you. Keep in mind they MUST have read your vision and have a clear understanding of where you would like to go with it. Be careful of choosing people because they are friends, family, or someone you like. The criterion is that they are as enthusiastic as you are in fulfilling the vision – this may not come from a friend, family member or person you admire.

Have a book to record everything that happens from now on, including the people, places, events, and insignificant moments. And do not forget to record your "Ron Moore" moments!

Then, put it into action. *Do it!* Take steps toward your purpose. Take small, measurable, intentional, and achievable steps. But do it TODAY!

Rashidi's life underwent a remarkable transfor-mation with just a simple request, leading him to uncover four key principles that, when implemented, revealed a delightful window of opportunity. Explore further to learn more...

Caregivers DO Matter

In the bustling city of Philadelphia, there resided a peaceful, patient man named Rashidi. His life took an unexpected twist when he found himself in charge of caring for his now 103-year-old aunt.

During one of his frequent "drive-by" visits, while working in the area, Rashidi voiced a surprising request. "Hey Auntie, can I stay here with you for a few weeks until I get settled?" Rashidi inquired having recently sold his home and was looking for a place outside of the city.

"My goodness, of course you can. It will be great for both of us; we'll be company for each other for the time being," his aunt replied.

Little did he know those few weeks would turn into an ever-challenging new chapter in life. Spending more than a few casual minutes on an occasional visit revealed the true condition of his aunt; another unassuming senior with dementia. After this unsettling revelation, there was no way he could leave her living alone.

Over the course of eleven years, Rashidi dedicated himself entirely to her well-being, with the support of a local hospice and palliative care agency. He, like so many others, learned to live with the unpredictable and sometimes unspeakable events that often accompany caring for someone with compromised mental capacity.

When Rashidi first stepped into the role of a caregiver, he was overwhelmed with a whirlwind of negative emotions. The weight of the responsibility felt crushing, and he often battled feelings of loneliness and helplessness.

He never counted on the shear enormity of his aunt's unpredictable behavior, the unbelievable occurrences, (like leaving the home late at night, being returned by the local police), or plain senseless decisions (like cooking everything in the freezer, thinking it was thanksgiving – in June). Yet, amidst this emotional storm, a glimmer of hope began to shine through.

As days turned into weeks and weeks into years, Rashidi embarked on a profound inner journey. He learned to acknowledge and channel his emotions, using them as motivation to make thoughtful decisions for his aunt's welfare. Gradually, his perspective shifted from despair to determination and clarity.

With a change in his thinking, serendipity began to play a role in turning the tide during this journey. He crossed paths with Melvin, a fellow caregiver who had left a lucrative career to look after his aging parents. The two found solace in each other's company, sharing stories of triumphs and challenges that resonated deeply.

Despite never meeting face-to-face, their conversations were filled with empathy and understanding. They would check in on each other with genuine concern, offering words of comfort and support through life's ups and downs.

Soon, others became aware of and joined the circle of support. What started as a lonely journey down a never-ending road turned into a path of purpose and fulfillment.

Inspired by the impactful dialogues with Melvin, Rashidi began jotting down his thoughts and reflections. What started as a personal journal evolved into a supportive community called "The Guiltless Caregiver," (www.TheGuiltlessCaregiver.com) where caregivers could find solace and share their experiences without fear of judgment.

With a newfound sense of purpose, Rashidi poured his heart into creating a book titled "Why Won't They Just Die, A Caregiver's Call for Help." This moving narrative shed light on the silent struggles of caregivers, serving as a beacon of guidance for those currently in the caregiving role or considering taking it on.

Through the process of reflective thinking, directed emotions and feelings, communicating positively, and writing his visions and future plans, Rashidi underwent a profound transformation. He no longer viewed caregiving as a burden but as a sacred calling, a chance to extend kindness and compassion to those in need. His mantra, "Caregivers DO Matter," resonated far and wide, advocating for the recognition and honor of these unsung heroes.

As Rashidi's story unfolded, he became a beacon of hope in a world clouded by uncertainties, inspiring others to acknowledge the crucial role of caregivers and the significant impact they have on shaping lives. By celebrating the worth of caregiving, Rashidi not only found his purpose but also paved the way for others to follow, championing the cause of care and kindness in a world that craves it.

Through his journey of challenges and victories, Rashidi displayed the untold tale of resilience, empathy, and unwavering commitment that lies within every caregiver's heart. By implementing the four keys to fulfilling his purpose, thinking, feeling, speaking, and writing, the doing happened effortlessly. By sharing his narrative, he planted the seeds of change, nurturing a future where caregivers are acknowledged, their voices heard, and their contributions cherished. Yes, "Caregivers DO Matter," indeed.

(www.CaregiversDoMatter.com)

"Just DO IT!"

*"Live Life with Purpose
& Passion!"*

Conclusion

Now that you have a clear and practical process that will enable you to discover and fulfill your purpose, what now? What are you going to do with this information? Are you just going to give it the traditional nod of approval, agreeing with the truth you have learned? Will you resolve to apply this process or wait until you carve out time from your busy schedule? Perhaps this is yet another "self-help" book you've read, but haven't "plugged in" to find your passion for life or purpose for living.

Take time to examine your methods and motives for living. Ask yourself, "Have I been living just to see what I can gain for myself and my own interests? Am I living to make a difference in what I have rather than in who I am? Am I going through my day seeking opportunities to be served by others rather than to serve others? Am I living in fear of the future, paralyzed by my past? Do I desire to leave a legacy of peace and goodwill for those who follow me in this life?"

Some of us may be uninformed or ill informed concerning our reason for existing. Perhaps we have gotten so caught up in the process of life that we have neglected the purpose for which we exist. How many needy people have we overlooked, passed by, failed to communicate with, missed speaking a kind word to, or refused a pleasant passing glance because we were so engrossed in our own thoughts and circumstances? We all have experienced hurt, such as having regret over things we've done or not done and situations that have happened beyond our control.

We allow these things to become reasons why we cannot help others. We rely on them as we do a crutch for a broken leg. But we fail to realize that there may come a day when no excuse is acceptable. One day, we will need a helping hand or a kind word to get us through our own crisis. After all, we are all in need of a human touch sometime.

Still, we tend to focus on our own needs and desires, and not others. We seem to ascribe to the belief that our purpose is to serve self first and foremost, and then serve others. Unfortunately, some never get past themselves. Even the best intentions of sincere individuals, while making an attempt, find themselves questioning the "wisdom" of putting others' interests in front of their own.

So, what now? How to we move from where we are to the place that will enable us to better fulfill our divine purpose in life? What do we do to start the process of thinking, feeling, speaking, and writing?

Examine yourself

A good place to start is with yourself. Examine yourself first. Ask yourself, "Why do I want to fulfill my true purpose in life? Is the way I'm living making a difference in the world around me? Am I being who I am created to be? If not, why not? Am I seeking purpose to gain more for me? Am I seeking purpose to satisfy the need within myself or the need in others? Do I want a better job, business or career; more money or more recognition? Do I care that others are smiling, comforted, or better off for having me cross their path?"

Mark 8:34-36 says: *"And Jesus called [to Him] the throng with His disciples and said to them, If anyone intends to come after Me, let him deny himself [forget, ignore, disown, and lose sight of himself and his own interests] and take up his cross, and [joining Me as a disciple and siding with My party] follow with Me [continually, cleaving steadfastly to Me].*

For whoever wants to save his [higher, spiritual, eternal] life, will lose it [the lower, natural, temporal life which is lived only on earth]; and whoever gives up his life [which is lived only on earth] for My sake and the Gospel's will save it [his higher, spiritual life in the eternal kingdom of God].

For what does it profit a man to gain the whole world, and forfeit his life [in the eternal kingdom of God]?" (Amplified Bible)

Now, ask yourself these questions: "How will I be remembered by others after I transition from this physical realm? Will I be remembered as one who only did what was convenient, comfortable, profitable, or affordable? Will anyone remember when I gave of myself to meet the physical, emotional or spiritual need of another?"

Is fulfilling your purpose in life on hold while you ponder all the things you would, could or should do if only you had the opportunity? Is fulfilling your purpose next in line after all the things you want to experience, finish or gain in life first?

Many individuals, like you, have "died with the music still in them." Burial grounds are filled with the bones of those with delayed intentions, unfulfilled dreams, and misappropriated greatness.

Many may say, "But I do not want to be great." This likely is due to a misunderstanding of the difference between being great and being famous. Not all famous people are great, nor are all great people famous. Fame is determined by the number of people by which you are known; greatness is determined by how well you have served others.

"Everyone has the power for greatness, not for fame but for greatness, because greatness is determined by service."

–Martin Luther King, Jr.

"As human beings, our greatness lies not so much
in being able to remake the world – that is the myth of the
atomic age – as in being able to remake ourselves."

–Mahatma Gandhi

"The greatest among you must be a servant."
–Jesus of Nazareth, (Matthew 23:11)

Examine your relationships

How do you relate to others? Are people attracted to you, tolerate you or run away when they see you coming? Are your friends simply acquaintances or are they truly close friends? Are you a good friend to anyone other than yourself? Are you willing to ask those you know if you are truly a friend? 3If you were to ask others what they think of you, will you be satisfied with their answers?

How much time do you spend thinking about what others have done to you or not done for you? How often do you consider why your phone or doorbell doesn't ring? Do people relate to you out of love or fear? "I better do this for him, so I won't hear it later."

Do you force your will, manipulate, coerce or use guilt in relating with others? What is your purpose in having those persons in your life?

There is a saying that goes, "You can fool some of the people, all of the time; all of the people, some of the time; but you can't fool all the people all the time." My clever addition to this quip would be: "And you can't fool God at all!"

Your purpose and intentions with others will be discovered sooner or later. You may feel that you are sincere in your relationships, but many sincere people have been sincerely wrong.

This is not to say that you should be concerned with what others think of your relationships, but there should be some honest people around you who will tell you the truth about you, in a loving and palatable way. Most times, we wait until we are fed up or disappointed and blurt out the most negative thoughts we've kept bottled up.

These can often be reflections of the other person's realization of themselves. "You always want your way," nearly always means the person saying it always wants their way and this time didn't get it because of you. "I don't think you like me," means "I don't like myself, so why should you."

Examine your spiritual life

How is your spiritual life? Are you aware of the presence of the Creator in all that you say and do? Do you want a deeper relationship or would you rather pay periodic homage to the Sovereign God to appease Him? Do you want Him to guide your life and reveal your reason for existing? Are you willing to give up and give in to what may truly be your reason for being created ON PURPOSE?

Are you satisfied with the way you are living every day? Are you grateful for all the people, places, events, and experiences you are privileged to have?

Now that you know, take every measure available to condition your mind to think positive thoughts. Get to know your own feelings and emotions, and make an effort to control them. Speak deliberately and positively, especially regarding yourself and your purpose.

Take time to put effort into writing your plans and purposes. Read them over and make adjustments as needed. Get help when you get stuck. Surround yourself with like-minded individuals who will cheer you on toward your goals.

Look everywhere for signs that speak to your spirit. Note the things that make you feel passionate about life. This is your life and your responsibility to live it.

Last but not least, get to know the Creator as personally and intimately as you can. Spend time quietly listening from within to hear the still, small voice with a personal message that only you can hear. Respond in your own personal and unique way, but always with joy, gratitude and love.

Examine others' lives

It's encouraging to know that the road toward fulfilling your purpose has been traveled by many before you. You have a "cloud of witnesses" that can testify that although the road was rough, they made it; and you can, too.

Learn from others' thousands of examples of courage and strength to fulfill their purpose, in spite of insurmountable obstacles. Of course we can all note examples throughout history and around the world, but there are many ordinary people who have extraordinary achievements in our own backyards.

What now? What excuse do you have NOT to live your life ON PURPOSE? It is not dependent on circumstances or situations. You have all the time and resources you need right here, right now. You are unique and wonderfully made. You are created for greatness. The world is waiting for you to emerge as that tremendous, caring, enthusiastic, positive, impacting person you are created to be.

Begin *Thinking, Feeling, Speaking, and Writing* on purpose and you will soon discover you too can experience the kind of life that you have desired deep inside and deserve to live. **Get started today!**

THINK FEEL SPEAK WRITE- DO

Footnotes

1. Definitions at the beginning of each chapter:Dictionary.com. (2011).
Retrieved March 2011, from http://dictionary.reference.com

Thoughts Can Make You Sick
1. Ygoy.com – Health & Lifestyle Updates. (2011). How pains and
diseases originate from our negative thoughts – mind therapy.
Retrieved March 2011, from http://www.ygoy.com/index.php/how-pains-
and-diseases-originate-from-our-negative-thoughts-mind-therapy

Emotions and Feelings Are Related to Thought
1. Pettinelli, Mark. (2008). The psychology of emotions, feelings and
thoughts. (4th ed). Mark Pettinelli.

2. Buzzle.com – Intelligent Life on the Web. (2000-2010, 2011). List of
human emotions. Retrieved March 2011, from http://www.buzzle.com/
articles/list-of-human-emotions.html

Words Can Heal
1. Lomax, John. A., (1910). Cowboy songs and other frontier ballads.
New York: Sturgis and Walton

2. Stevie Wonder. (1973). Living for the city. On Innervisions. [record].
Detroit: Tamla (Motown) Records

It Takes Work to Change Your Mind
1. E., W. (2011). W. e. vine's new testament greek grammar and
dictionary. Thomas Nelson, Inc.

2. Dictonary.com. (2011). Retrieved March 2011, from http://dictionary.
reference.com/browse/abide

Feel Your Way to Fulfilling Your Purpose
1. Significance of Colors in Feng Shui Practice. The Spiritual Feng Shui.
Retrieved March 2011, from http://www.thespiritualfengshui.com/
feng-shui-color.php

Contact R. Lee Moore, Sr.

For Book Signings &
Speaking Engagements:

RLeeMooreSr@gmail.com
(844) 246-2200

www.**RonaldLeeMooreSr**.com

R. Lee Moore, Sr.
295 E. Swedesford Road, #288
Wayne, PA 19087

www.one**creative**mindllc.com

www.ingramcontent.com/pod-product-compliance
Lightning Source LLC
Chambersburg PA
CBHW041627140626
46547CB00031B/1168